SELLING
WITH
LOVE

SELLING WITH LOVE

EARN WITH INTEGRITY & EXPAND YOUR IMPACT

JASON MARC CAMPBELL

SELLING WITH LOVE
Earn with Integrity and Expand Your Impact

ISBN   978-1-5445-2689-8   *Hardcover*

      978-1-5445-2687-4   *Paperback*

      978-1-5445-2688-1   *Ebook*

I'd like to dedicate this book to my mother and father.
They brought me into this world and shaped me into
the man I am now. I am eternally grateful.

CONTENTS

INTRODUCTION

"Wow, I can't believe how selfish you are by charging people so little for your event."

I remember saying this as a guest on a podcast where the host was struggling to sell her event. She was shocked. She had never thought of herself as a selfish person. She was out there, doing her best to serve the people. Yet, as she explained to me the challenges she faced with selling tickets to her event, she also felt bad because she was struggling to stay true to her conflicting values. She wanted to pay the speakers a fair fee out of integrity. She recognized the value of their content. But she was barely breaking even already. She couldn't run ads for her event, and she didn't want to raise the price of her tickets. Her reason? "I don't want to make my fans pay too much."

That's where I was quick to intercept. To assume your fans are going to pay too much is to lack clarity on the impact you'll be making on their lives. This comes from confusion on what problems you will solve for them and a lack of confidence in the product you'll deliver. It's also because as business owners, coaches, or salespeople, we often choose comfort over conversion.

We talked some more. I explained to her that even though she was trying to be considerate to her fans, she wasn't thinking about how to maximize their benefit from her event. If she had truly been understanding of their needs, she would've realized that it didn't compromise her values at all to raise the fees of the speakers. If the ticket price increased, she could give her fans the best possible content, making her event worth the money. More importantly, a better event would justify the time and faith her fans had already decided to give to her. In the end, she realized that her event was incredible, her clients would get genuine transformation, and the impact would be incredible. We used her current internal struggles as a way to authentically communicate to her clients why the price for the event was about to go up—significantly.

She still had weeks to go before the event started. A simple email was sent out to her list of potential buyers:

"Hey, fans,

As you know, I put together this event by making sure you get an amazing transformation and truly find the solutions to the struggles you face right now. As such, I've gone out and found some of the best speakers. I will be making sure they get paid well so they share their best content (as opposed to simply delivering a tease to their content and telling you to buy more). This is why I want to raise the price of the event. Because I care about bringing to you the best experience you've ever had at a live event, and I know this to be true. Now, because you are a fan, I'd love to give you one more chance to buy the last ten tickets at the current price. After this, prices will double, and it will still be a bargain for what you'll be getting at the event. And if it's a bargain you enjoy, then the best one you can get is by getting your ticket right now before I sell out. You don't want to miss this, and as always, you can always get a refund by the end of the event if it wasn't the best experience of your life."

Not bad? She sold out the event. She was able to raise the prices, too. And from what I know, no one asked for a refund.

This woman is one of many individuals and companies that have worked with me at solving a key issue: how do I continue to make the *impact* I want to make in the world and keep the *integrity* in my way of selling?

People come to me usually with a sense of defeat. They started out with an idealistic view on how their business was going to be different. Yet, the pressures of the market have made it difficult. They are at a crossroads, thinking that their values must be compromised. They must start to sell in manipulative ways like the "other" people in their industry.

I get excited when they come to me for help because I get to show them that there is another way. A better way. You can have it all.

I've loved sales for as long as I can remember. From the very first jobs I had as a teenager until now, running a consulting company on sales and marketing, I've always had a "strange" love for selling. Everywhere I've worked, I've been referred to as the guy who can sell anything. Yet, the way I do it is a little different. It comes with a large portion of integrity. Call it a sense of humanity in the process. This is what I wish to show you along the way.

Over the last decade, I've worked and been involved in some capacity with Mindvalley. This personal growth development company has been a big part of my journey. It's where I've tested and refined my ideas on selling with love. It's also helped me grow in so many ways through their personal growth programs. I use them as examples through this book not because they are a perfect organization (no one is). It is because so many moments have allowed me to apply what I teach in this book, which you'll be able to learn from and apply in your life. I've been on the sales team and the executive team. I've run events and worked with the top authors in the personal growth space. Through these experiences and so many more, I find myself sharing this message with you.

I've also been massively taken advantage of as an individual. I'm talking about being featured in an infomercial at a national level, giving support to an organization that scammed me. I've seen what sales can do at its worse.

Yet my love for sales remains. I'm hoping to share the lessons from the "good" and the "bad." All of it has wisdom to help you grow.

When you see sales as the amazing tool that it is—a way of getting people to take action on what is genuinely believed to be a great investment for them—you can see it as a source of transformation in the world.

Our society is a reflection of what has been sold to everyone, including all the ideas we endorse, the products we use, the services we subscribe to, the politicians who get elected, and the businesses that grow and thrive. Everything that is alive and growing in our social and economic spheres is a product of a sales pitch that was successful or not.

I remember when the internet was becoming a mainstream thing. People were commenting on the glory of having access to all this new information. They were saying it would bring an end to salespeople. Yet, now we face a new problem that only salespeople can fill: we are overwhelmed with information. The salesperson helps the buyer make these decisions so they aren't paralyzed in decision making.

See, there's nothing intrinsically "good" or "bad" about working in sales. At the end of the day, it's a tool. But it's also a skill that is now more powerful and necessary to the functioning of society than ever. If you have a beautiful vision for how you want to improve the world, it would be a grave mistake *not* to learn about sales.

Now, if you've ever felt resistance to sell, maybe it's because you freeze up about the idea of being an "aggressive" salesperson. Maybe you've seen your business fail to reach the growth it could experience, because you'd rather do everything else before selling. If that's the case, this book is for you.

You can only imagine how many business owners, coaches, and regular people I've met who hold themselves back because they think, "Yeah, I just don't like sales."

We are all salespeople, whether we like it or not. Sales is the flow of the world. And when you embrace it as opposed to resist it, you'll have much more alignment, abundance, and authenticity in who you are and in the impact you can make on this planet.

This book was written with a goal in mind. See, when I went through my own encounters with sales, I had my good and bad experiences. One of the less fun rides, as you'll learn in the book, landed me as the face of a national campaign in Canada, which prompted people to sign up to the same scam I was duped by. It left me feeling so furious and led me to get extremely passionate about one thing:

If more people who are working at doing great things in the world learn to sell properly, we will finally get to see that world emerge faster than ever.

By the end of this book, you'll have hopefully learned what changes need to happen within yourself to get rid of any guilt or shame from your sales experiences, because you'll know that you are truly making an impact and serving the client. And when you get there, everything will change for the better.

I want you to imagine the following way of doing sales. Imagine that you have become absolutely clear on your potential impact. If you are an entrepreneur, you are clear on what happens to the world when your business grows. You know what happens to the people who work for you, the message you spread, and the products you sell. I'm talking about every single stakeholder in the process.

Let's use Mindvalley as an example. I've had the chance to be a part of the organization for seven years. I'm very proud to have been a part of the goal they set from the start: to positively impact one billion people through transformational education.

How did we translate this into the way we did business? Well, it required a mindset shift. Revenue and profits of course are necessary, yet during a strategy meeting, we would start with purpose, values, and mission. Starting with this ensured that every decision made would answer the ultimate question: Why? Why do anything? The answer: to support the impact goal of reaching one billion people.

It would make everyone focus on solving true problems in our industry. For example, online learning had a very low rate of success for people who paid and enrolled. How do we fix that? We initiated product innovations that would make this improvement happen and be measurable. This attitude would trickle down the organization so we would all be empowered to think this way. Impact first.

Every time I got a chance to work on a project, I'd have clarity of purpose on why it was important to deliver at a high quality. Everything I did mattered. I've launched products that generated millions of dollars. I've worked with incredible teams to sell out one-month-long events in cities such as Barcelona and Tallinn. It's been truly an honor to be a part of this team to make it happen.

Can you imagine the power you have when you take the time to sell to your employees with love? You inspire them to deliver their best; you get them engaged. You recruit the best.

This also translated in how clients would purchase. Sales numbers would skyrocket as everything was tied to a grand vision. A purpose. Buyers had an understanding of the movement and impact that fueled every dollar they spent.

Through this book, I'll share more about how important this clarity of impact is and how it will translate to feeling amazing about every sale you make.

With this clarity, you explode in motivation to do what is required to grow. That is a love-based reason for existence. And you'll learn how to love your impact, too.

Now let's look at the individual customer/client/buyer. Imagine being so crystal clear on who this person is and what they are looking for. Imagine you know their daily struggles, their fears, their aspirations, their limitations, and their potential. You know what they dream about. And you absolutely know the problems they have and how motivated they are to see themselves without that problem.

I can only think of my client Lucy. She is a mother of a nineteen-year-old, yet her relationship with her daughter isn't as good as she would hope. She owns a small flower shop that is doing okay, but it's hard work. She loves watching the movie *The Secret* and is very aware of the law of attraction. She has, however, felt like the law of attraction has never really worked the way she expected. She got divorced many years ago and has gotten "okay" with being alone. This lingering sadness has become a normal thing. Yet deep down, she knows there is more to life than this. And getting a break or a breakthrough is really all she wishes right now. It's been so long since someone has believed in her; she now craves it.

Do you know a Lucy in your life? I feel like I do. After speaking to so many people during my market research to sell a product on energy healing, I started to paint a beautiful picture of this ideal target client. See, when you get clear on your client, you feel their pain. You know the solution brings love, joy, and more. And you will be unstoppable. You'll learn how to love your client, which is key.

And what about the product? Could you imagine having a product so good, so amazing, and priced so right that when you need to explain it to people, you can't hold yourself back from getting so excited and enthusiastic about it? The person sees the glow in your eyes. They get excited, too! You know, from the bottom of your heart, that this product is really designed to make the world a better place, and they are getting the very best of what it could possibly be.

The importance of loving your product cannot be understated. And you'll see exactly how to shape your current product into something that will make it so easy to sell that you'll never see it the same.

You hear of all these sales tactics that exist and they all seem like effort. Plus, they seem manipulative. Not anymore. When you understand that your impact, the client, and the product are so aligned within a place of love, you won't be able to hold yourself back from actually loving the process of selling. Getting on a sales call? Hell yeah! Posting on social media? Let's go! New advertising campaign? Product launch? A book on closing a sale better? Bring. It. On. You'll start to love the process so much because you'll know that when you speak the language required for people to make powerful decisions, you'll have zero resistance.

This is the case for liking sales. As a matter of fact, by the end of this book, you will *love* sales.

A BOOK ABOUT SMALL BUSINESSES

I want to acknowledge something you'll find throughout this book. Most examples presented throughout relate to small businesses. It is, in fact, the key market in which I see individuals having reluctance in sales. Regardless of whether you are working in a corporation, the government, or even a nonprofit, you'll see that the examples used in this book will support you in your work. Getting the right sales mindset is the foundation for everything else you look to achieve in life. Get ready to dive in and enjoy.

PART 1

LET'S LOOK AT SALES FROM A DIFFERENT LENS

I FOUND IT IDEAL TO SPLIT THIS BOOK INTO TWO MAJOR PARTS. KNOW THAT selling with love is the ultimate goal of this book. But if our beliefs and ideas around sales don't even open to the possibility of not hating sales, it will be quite difficult to sell with love.

When you pick up this book, I don't know where you are starting from and what your relationship to sales currently is. What I will say is that if any hesitance, reluctance, or disdain for sales as an industry exists, then this section is going to be eye-opening for you.

First, we begin at the foundation of sales and start looking at it from a whole new perspective. Once this has been established, you will then have room to grow into someone who can sell from a place of love (more on this in Part 2).

I've created a sales mindset assessment to give you an idea of where you are starting from and I encourage you to complete this test before reading the book. You can find it at jasonmarccampbell.com/test.

Once you finish the test and read the book, you'll be able to review your results and see the progress you've made.

With that being said, let's get started.

CHAPTER 1

WHY YOU HATE SALES

I COULDN'T BELIEVE IT WHEN PEOPLE STARTED MESSAGING ME saying, "Hey, Jason! We saw you on TV last night!" I'm not one to be shy on camera—that wasn't the problem. But one day, I found myself featured on a series of infomercials that started running across Canada. Once again, this wouldn't be so bad if it wasn't for a simple fact: everything great I was saying about the program was a lie. I was in the middle of taking my first doses of Prozac after being diagnosed with depression caused by stress.

Rewind a few months. I'm sitting at a restaurant with my two best friends from university. We've just graduated and we are faced with a "now what?" scenario. I've just come back from a seminar on how to buy US real estate and become rich in the process. I'm so excited to get started and pay the fees to get into the mentorship program. It's $20,000. We all put our money together and get started. Next stop: Orlando, Florida.

We meet up with our "mentor" who takes us to visit properties. This is back in 2010. The market is flooded with short sales and foreclosures (banks have taken over property from people who failed to pay). Our mentor encourages us to put an offer on every property, reassuring us that his cousin will give us the money to buy them all. This sounds too good to be true!

Shortly after that amazing day, we are brought into the recording studio to share our excitement. This very clip is what gets featured in the infomercial.

This was before I realized that the cousin was *not* going to fund the deals. Before I learned that what we learned from our "mentor" was risky and not safe. And before I could see through the smoke and mirrors that were put in place to record that very testimonial they wanted to use.

A few days after, once we had properties under contract, we could not reach this "cousin"; he disappeared. The lawyers we were recommended had complaints against them for fraud. The very foundation of the knowledge I was taught was wrong. And now, as the whole reality set in, it was not pretty.

I got scammed.

It was painful enough to know that I lost time and money. Worse was that I had involved people, including family members, who had given me tens of thousands of dollars. I realized everything I thought

I knew was a lie. My enthusiasm in that infomercial was recorded just a few months before I knew. Now thousands of other Canadians would start to buy into the same crap. It was a lot to take in at twenty-one years old. This was not how things were supposed to happen.

Why do people fall for scams? Very rarely does anyone look back and say, "Oh yeah, there were no signs." Instead, you can clearly trace back all the ignored evidence. Everything you ignored as you were blinded by hopes and confidence. Close by was a salesperson, telling you everything would be okay.

A SLICK REPUTATION

If you've never been scammed before, maybe you've been in many encounters with a salesperson where you felt manipulated, cheated, and/or simply lied to. Sometimes it's not about what they say but about what they don't say.

"Oh, they never told me that my subscription had a fifty dollar cancellation fee."

"Looks like that final price didn't include all these extra costs like service fees."

"Oh wait, the contract you signed has locked you in and you can't make any changes."

This goes beyond our own personal experiences. Think about all the cultural memes that exist in the world today. You don't need to think too much about a used car salesperson, Wall Street stock-broker, or real estate agent to have a very precise image of exactly what personality types these people have. More importantly, you probably have a certain emotion that comes up as well. For most people, that emotion isn't very positive.

If you are part of the conversation on social media, there's a whole influencer culture that exists. Promoting any kind of product for a buck. I think it gets even more interesting when I walk through shopping malls in Southeast Asia and see ads for fast food joints with an endorsement by a famous football player (soccer player, I mean). How is this happening? Are people just selling out?

Then you have this whole "get rich quick" culture online. Young marketers telling you the next big secret that only they know. The program they want you to buy is to learn how to make lots of money quickly and easily. Similar to what I found myself purchasing…only to find the program had questionable methods.

I've run workshops and done talks where I ask people to tell me what words come up when I say "salesperson."

Some answers I get: "bad," "slimy," "manipulative," "slick," "evil," and "annoying." I also get "powerful" and "movers and shakers." Our ideas around sales are highly charged, especially in American culture.

Our media also reinforces these ideas when you think of shows like *Mad Men* or *The Wolf of Wall Street* (or simply *Wall Street* for those of you who prefer the Gordon Gekko reference). I could list so many more shows that paint the picture of these sleazy, manipulative salespeople. Yet, there are also communities formed around people inspired by these sales figures and hope to be "just like them." I know I've watched my share of videos that made me look up to these salespeople, regardless of the true impact they had on society.

As tragic as it is when you look at the impact this has on the buyers and the world, there is something appealing about the process. Many individuals rush to this opportunity to make lots of money fast. Instant wealth and glamour. With promises for riches, status, fun, and having a powerful sense of control over your destiny, this is hard to resist.

These people seem to be the reason our world is going down the drain. Let me give you a final example of a little someone you might have heard of: Donald J. Trump. Salesperson? You bet. Love him? We all do. If we didn't, he wouldn't grab our attention the way he does and get to places that seemed impossible.

And that's the interesting part. With all of the examples of "famous" salespeople, they are still in power. They capture our attention. They are winning the game. As much as we have these negative ideas around all these stereotypes and references, they still sell. And we still give them the power to do so.

WHY DO WE BUY FROM
BAD SALESPEOPLE?

Growing up, I've witnessed firsthand what happened when a slick sales guy was at my father's swimming pool shop. Everyone hated him. He was disrespectful to everyone, causing drama in the office. And then it was revealed that he had started his own company and was selling other products by himself to fill his pockets with even more money.

But wow, he could sell.

People were buying! Like ridiculously more than any other salesperson ever hired. As a small business, it was impossible to get rid of him (or so it seemed), since the growth was tied to his performance. And he knew it, too.

So why is it that people like this, and all the examples from before, still thrive today?

In an age where there is an overload of information, people are looking for a confident, reliable source of information that can help them make a decision without feeling trapped by the paradox of choice.

Think about it. You want to buy a used car. You start to get close to what kind of car you want. You start looking online for reviews. You look on websites like Autotrader or Google "used cars" in your area. What do you find? *So many* used cars available! Oh my god, how do you move forward? You start looking by price, and for everything that you look at, a little voice at the back of your head says, "Yeah, but is it really the best one? What if you make a bad decision?"

And you freeze. Used car salespeople need you to simply come and walk the lot. It's game over once you get there, because it's never about the car you call about. It's about them being able to show you a car and say, "*This* is the perfect one for you." And hearing that is a relief from the paralysis of endlessly browsing online.

And if this is a good dealership, they will have all the programs in place to remove all the fears you might have with buying the car. "Six-month warranty," "You can drive it for a week and bring it back," "If you find another car for cheaper, we will pay you the difference." You get the picture.

When a salesperson comes to you with that confidence and gives you reassurance that the decision you want to make is the perfect one… it feels so good. I mean yes, a little voice might be telling you that he may be lying to you. But you ignore it. You just want the pain of indecision to go away. You want to move forward. And that salesperson is trained in understanding human psychology and emotions, while you are severely underprepared to handle this. It's not an even match.

That's why I say that as much as you hate those salespeople, you also love them. But it's a dysfunctional relationship.

Now, I promise by the end of this book, you'll have healed those parts of you that fall for these bad sales situations. You'll understand exactly how to have a better relationship with sales. The way these bad salespeople get you by giving you hope is not a bad thing. You just need more clarity on what the ideal looks like. And even more, you need evidence that it actually is true.

UNDERSTANDING THE BAD SALESPERSON

Before we get to that, I think it's key to understand these "bad" salespeople a little more. I mean, why is it that they would seek to manipulate other human beings for the sake of closing a sale? Are they born as evil people destined to wreak havoc on all others? It's much simpler than you think. Fact is, blaming these salespeople is not going to solve the problem. Understanding them will bring much more light to the issue.

Scarcity and fear are the source of all bad sales. And abundance solves much of the problem.

I remember walking the streets of Thailand when a vendor came to me with a series of watches to sell. He showed me these items with some very recognizable logos on them. He quickly assured me, "This is a real Rolex. I'll give you a good price. Amazing quality item. Perfect condition." *Right.* As much as I'd love to believe this incredible offer for a fifty-dollar Rolex, I knew the product was fake, and this person was lying to me.

I love this example because most people can recognize that the vendor was clearly lying. Yet, let's take a moment to go deeper. Why does the vendor lie? I mean, something must motivate this person to lie to another human being so openly.

Is it simply because this person was born evil? I find that very hard to believe.

On the other side of the equation, there are the wealthy people who keep doing what might be considered questionable. I do want to clarify that having material "abundance" isn't the whole picture, as people who are constantly chasing more and more money can often feel like there is never enough. There is no point of satisfaction. Only a desire for more...and at any cost. This can make the billionaire still operate from a place of scarcity.

People are victims of circumstances and conditioning. I don't want to take away any personal responsibility from the bad salespeople. But I want you to recognize how the fear and scarcity in the world affects everyone. It could make anyone take decisions that will not serve the greater good. It's hard to blame the Thailand vendor for conducting such a business. It's much more realistic to see someone who needs to generate income, feed their family, and get out of poverty, doing what they know best to make a difference in their own life. Their model of reality is closer to "I need to go out there and hustle to change my personal circumstances" than "I need to manipulate this person." If telling you "This Rolex is real" is what will sell more, so be it. Don't take it personally; the person is simply doing their best.

Between this whole idea of good versus bad sales is a whole spectrum of gray area. My goal will be to push for more awareness of impact throughout your sales process. When you become aware, you can continue to grow.

I've made sales from the purest intent when I was younger. I remember going to a training event in Atlanta, Georgia, where people were learning to become entrepreneurs. I was invited to be a guest to witness and support their sales processes. I found myself working with people who were watching the event from their homes through the livestream, and I was ready to sell the program the moment the pitch was made. I got excited, had faith in the program, and was given a clear list of benefits to support the sales. I got on the phone with people calling in for information. I would get enthusiastic and follow the process. "Will that be Visa or Mastercard?" "This is the perfect program for you. We can start now." "Why don't we run the card now and save your spot, and you'll have a few days to think about it after."

Great closing lines. Effective. We generated record sales numbers. But when I think back now, a question I ask myself is: How much time did I take to make sure what I was selling was great? Valuable? Impactful? I gambled on my faith in the author to sell what they told me, yet every sale I made had a huge risk. That risk was to the buyer and to my integrity.

Learning from this, now I get to make more conscious sales that align with my values.

SOCIOPATHIC SALES TRAINING: YES, IT HAPPENS

Is there any reason to study sales at all if you want to do good in the world? If you have this book in your hands, surely this isn't the first time you studied sales? Why did you resist a sales training you've seen in the past? Did it feel aligned? Did you get excited about implementing all their ideas?

This is where I see a fundamental problem with what exists on the bookshelves and in sales training role models. It's often looking at sales as an "us versus them" scenario, where the salesperson must win, and in exchange, the buyer must...lose. It speaks a language that doesn't support the impact you want to make or the people you want to serve. Think this language is important? Let me quote a few conversations that are very common in sales training:

"Make sure the potential buyer isn't a TWA."

TWA: time-wasting asshole.

"We need to set up a trip-wire offer to get the person to convert."

Trip-wire offer: a small purchase to get someone to become a client. This will make them easier to convert to a higher offer in the future. In military combat, a trip wire is a hidden detonator activated by the foot of an unwitting victim.

It's quite difficult to see the "love" in selling when the result is a relationship built on this kind of hostile language. Yet, there's a reason to use some of these techniques: they work. They absolutely do work.

A key idea about sales is that it isn't a rational process. The rationality is simply a checkmark in the process. The whole experience needs to be looked at from an emotional lens. Even though these examples might come across as cruel and manipulative, the problem is not in the technique itself but the self-centered language used.

Language can be changed. Instead of using terms like "trip wire," some marketers and salespeople have started to use the term "welcome mat" (thanks to Ryan Lee for the suggestion). See the difference in energy? One suggests conquering and destruction; the other is about taking care of your clients. Instead of writing someone off as a TWA, you can explore how to turn these nonbuyers into promoters by developing a process on how to handle them with respect (while being efficient).

Unfortunately, salespeople often learn about the negative TWA terms rather than how to come from a genuine position of helping people. Here is the problem: Most of the people who are focused on impact *and* integrity are not picking up the information they need. Most courses and books around sales have titles and marketing messaging that leave you thinking you will be able to manipulate people. Consequently, the salesperson who isn't concerned about the effects of their sales on the buyer can and will get the advantage because they will willingly learn this sales process. It will work to bring results but comes from a place of service to self, before acknowledging service to others. Again, the problem isn't the person; it's this idea that abundance can only come at the expense of others.

The message that most aspiring salespeople pick up: If you don't become successful, you'll be a loser and die alone. You are not enough. Work harder. The world is filled with winners and losers.

This can be stressful for purpose-aligned individuals, because it seems like to survive, you'll need to compromise on your values. But don't worry, there is another way.

WHAT TO EXPECT FROM
THIS BOOK

Just to be clear, I'm not asking you to absolutely *love* selling. I'm simply asking you to consider that you might like it. Just a little. It's totally possible if only you first suspend any judgment around sales and salespeople.

The ideas shared in this book will allow you to fix any problems you might have in selling. You'll find yourself embracing them from a position of abundance. Everyone you know you can help will truly be on board with your mission, get massive transformation from your product, and more.

Knowing how to sell will be incredibly useful to you. But first, I want you to absorb this message: Selling is neutral. It's like a handshake. It's innocent in and of itself. The positivity or negativity of selling is more about how you apply the skills and knowledge you have of selling with the awareness of the impact your sales make. See, it's very important that you suspend any negative associations with sales while reading this book, because if you don't, you will shut yourself off from alternate possibilities, not wanting to become something that you dislike. You will resist a different outcome. And you will not embrace its transformative potential.

The world is not without its problems. If I think about that time I got scammed, I had some very important choices to make on how I would tell the story in my head of what happened. Yes, I could play the victim. I could think, poor me, look at those bad people and what they did to me; it's not fair.

Interestingly enough, in the midst of so much trouble—being confused and having involved so many people I cared about in transactions I didn't understand—I pulled through by learning everything I could about the real estate transaction process. I had amazing people come to my life to help. (Tony Singleton, I will forever be grateful for your guidance through this time.) I read so many documents on tax implications for foreign owners of real estate; it was absolutely crazy. I ended up fixing all the deals that I got stuck with, got motivated to sell them to all the people the right way, and ended up making some money in the process. It was the biggest learning and growth period of my life when I look back at it.

Do I wish this on anyone? Of course not. I ended up building educational courses on the process so others wouldn't need to go through the same pain. And as for that scammy coach who lied to me, I don't speak to him or know what he is up to. Most likely, he is creating new unscrupulous ways to get people to give him money for new projects.

This is one of my biggest motivators in writing this book as well. Good companies, with good products need to learn how to outsell bad ones. And you'll learn how in the following chapters.

CHOOSE A BETTER STORY

Final note on my story of being scammed. Even if what happened to me was manipulative, the story I chose to tell myself was this: "Perhaps this person didn't know what I was capable of. They didn't know that to make me learn and grow, I had to be thrown so deep into the ocean that I'd have to learn to swim back. This person never realized they were the greatest teacher I ever had."

I've had to learn how to do cross-border real estate transactions myself to fix the problems. I've had to desperately find buyers and make the deals work. I had to learn the whole real estate transaction system to ensure everything was done right. The end result was flipping a bunch of properties for a profit and leaving my buyers with amazing deals that were renovated, rented, and cash flowing.

Whether his intention was pure or not doesn't matter. The story I tell myself is what is important. I invite you to look at any bad sales experience you've had. Instead of blaming the salesperson or shaming yourself, claim it as your life experience. Think about how much wiser and more aware it made you. That experience has sent you to exactly where you needed to go. To quote from the book *Conversations with God* by Neale Donald Walsch, "I've sent nothing but angels to you."

There is ultimate power in acknowledging this. As you step into this understanding and let go of the victimization of any past sales encounter you've had, you'll start to be able to consider that sales might actually be something you can do. You can like it. And eventually, you might even love it.

THE FEELING OF A GREAT SALE

Back when I was working for Mindvalley, I was at one of their flagship events called A-Fest. I had implemented many new initiatives in the company to embrace more engaged sales processes. In doing so, I took on a few leads and worked them through our pipeline to eventually get them to buy tickets to this event.

Here I was at the closing party in Jamaica, walking around the magical house where everyone was dressed for a scene that could only be described as the set of a new version of Alice in Wonderland (because yes, events require epic costume parties to happen for the closing). It's almost 1:00 a.m.; everyone is dancing. Some might even be a little tipsy. At this point, I'm relaxing and relieved that the event is quite successful, and I let myself enjoy the party as well.

A lady noticed me and started walking intensely toward me. I was confused because I had no idea who she was. Yet, her expression seemed to indicate that she knew I was one of the event managers. She asked me, "Are you Jason Campbell?"

Nervously, I answered. "Yes. How can I help?"

Here I'm thinking, maybe she has a complaint. Something happened and I need to take care of it. When running events, there are always problems. I thought I could relax for tonight.

"Oh, we need to talk. You're the guy who emailed and talked to me on the phone to sell me tickets to this event. You even texted me on WhatsApp when I ignored you! I've never had anyone persist this much."

I smile and relax instantly. I remember Leah now. We had not met in person, but I remember the effort I put into "closing" her to buy her ticket. It was a lengthy, fun process.

Leah continued, "And now, here I am, at 1:00 a.m. at this magical place in Jamaica, having the best time of my life. And it's all because of you. Thank you for selling me so persistently! My life changed because you didn't give up on me."

Is it possible to like sales? Well, when you do it from a place of love, you might get to a place where you get excitement from every sales encounter you have.

FOLLOW ALONG: IS IT RIGHT OR NOT?

Let me walk you through some previous sales experiences I've had. After each one, take a moment to think about how it made you feel.

In the first example, I remember leading the sales team at one of my early sales manager roles at a real estate agency. I had a small team of four people who were all working the phones. Our job was to call back all the people who had asked to see a property, get a price on their home, or get a list of available properties on the market. We were young, and we wanted to do our best to make money.

How would we get started for the day? What would be our "inspirational video"? We would regularly watch clips from shows like *Glengarry Glen Ross* in which Alec Baldwin reminds his failing sales agents that "coffee is only for closers" and that it takes "brass balls" to sell (literally taking a pair of brass balls from his suitcase to make a point). If it wasn't that scene, it was clips from *Boiler Room*, which documents young upcoming stockbrokers who worked for the infamous office of Jordan Belfort, aka the Wolf of Wall Street. We'd hear the speech from Ben Affleck sharing more words of wisdom such as, "They say money doesn't buy you happiness? Look at the fucking smile on my face," "We are here to get rich; we are not saving the manatees," and of course, "You will become the future Big Swinging Dicks of this organization."

After we would watch these clips, we would get on the phones and get people to book appointments with realtors, following specific scripts. It didn't matter much what the person said. We just needed to walk them through the flowchart.

1. "Do you rent or currently own your home?"

2. "Are you working with a realtor?"

3. "Are you planning to buy before you sell, or do you want to sell your home first?"*

*If person answers buy before, go to script item B.

We would call hundreds of people a day. Ring three times. If no answer, hang up, call again tomorrow. If the person said, "Please call me back in six months," we divided by two, and set a call back in three months. Objection? "I need to talk to my partner." Answer: "No problem. Let's pencil in a time, and if it doesn't work with your partner, we can reschedule."

It was a sales machine. There were few feelings. And the result? We sold lots of real estate. It was one of the top companies in the city. The whole system and process were so effective. We played our part in it and had clarity on what needed to be done.

Now, the question is: How do you feel when you hear this story? Do you think we were doing good or bad?

Let me add a detail. When someone called to see a property, we would be negatively evaluated if the person actually was given a chance to see that property. The goal was to get them into the office instead. One time, a potential client named John called and said, "I just want to see this property!" I replied, "No problem. Let's have you come to the office first and we can take you there afterward." I knew that more than likely, once they came to the office, we wouldn't take him to that property. My objective: Get him in the office. I did my job.

How do you feel now? Okay, another story.

This one lady—let's call her Cheryl—wanted to get a price on her home over the phone. I didn't tell her the price. I said someone needed to go to her house to give her that information. We had a rule:

Never give a price over the phone. Get the realtor in her house. I had my objective. She told me to call her again in two months. I called her over twenty-five times after one month. I left voice mails, lots of missed calls. She might have been avoiding my call. But I was relentless.

Is this getting to you yet? Let's see where these stories end.

Cheryl ended up listing and selling her house with our agency. When the agent asked why she decided to sign with us, she replied, "Well, I had this guy call me something like twenty times! So if you are that intense and persistent about wanting to get me as a client, I know you'll be the best to sell my house for top dollar."

John did come to the office as I told him. When he got here, he was educated on how to better choose properties, how to understand how the transaction process works, how to get preapproved for a mortgage/loan, and why this would save more money on his purchase. He had no obligation to continue to work with the agent. However, John decided to because he had never seen someone so organized on working with a buyer, and he could clearly see how working with this agent would save him time and money and make his life better. John didn't want to go see that property after all. It was too far from the school his kids wanted to go to. Most people see a property listed they think they like and want to go see, only to be disappointed once they visit (or even worse, loving the property but being so unprepared to make an offer that it is sold to someone else).

Let's dig a little more into why the "bad" salespeople seem to be so effective.

As we look for that confirmation that we've made the best possible decision in the current situation, an individual who can project a high level of confidence, enthusiasm, and relatability will push us to action. If you spend any time reading the books on sales that dissect human psychology, you'll quickly realize that you are not playing in a fair game. Imagine stepping into an ice-skating dance competition while putting on ice skates for the very first time. Anyone who's had any level of practice is sure to beat you. They don't need to be pros, just a little more practiced.

SALES IS A MAGNET FOR NARCISSISTS

Is it just a coincidence that many people in sales seem quite narcissistic? I wanted to dig deeper into this question. During a chat with Rebecca Zung, an attorney who specializes in dealing with narcissists at work, we looked at the trends to see what would attract a narcissist into sales. To be properly classified as a narcissist, they would be looking for constant external validation due to a diminished inner sense of value. This means getting people to think they are amazing, have lots of money, are powerful. Their sense of remorse, compassion to others, would be nonexistent.

Sounds pretty dangerous to me if you put this person in a toxic sales environment. I'm instantly reminded again of the superstar sales caricature from *The Wolf of Wall Street*, bringing all these dysfunctional, mostly young men together to defraud their investors, with no care for consequences.

A company operating with a leadership team with similar dysfunctions would be able to thrive with a team of these salespeople. Sales and profits would be high. And they would constantly try to find new "innocent" buyers to make the pitch.

Along a spectrum of dysfunction from not so good to terrible, the sales culture of the company will enable and attract these kinds of salespeople. I myself was attracted to this in my young days during a time I was looking for direction and felt filled with ambition.

I was young and innocent. Actually, young and ignorant is more accurate. I had drive, I had desire, and I wanted money and success. I was about to graduate university at the time and had explored my options. One was to work for the government. I had experience working there as an intern. Things moved slowly. The career path was set. Benefits were great. It seemed to tick all the right boxes. Yet, it didn't seem like it could make me rich. So I kept looking.

The second option was to explore companies at the school's job fairs. They had these management training programs. They showed me a path that was based on "meritocracy," with a great culture, but after years of working hard in this structure, you'd still be making a very average income.

I was impatient and frustrated. I got attracted to an opportunity in sales with real estate. The person recruiting me, the boss himself, started speaking a language that connected with me.

"You don't want to work hourly; commission-based allows you freedom to make as much as you want! You can easily make hundreds of thousands when you do this. You can start right now."

I was sold. And it became a numbers game. Having to do over one hundred calls per day. Measuring my ratio of calls to answering. Testing different times of the day. Following the scripts. Making the offers. Seeing how many people I could book. It was done effectively, yet lacked empathy. But it made me feel powerful, in control, and competent.

This would give me a rush. My perceived self-worth goes up. And you'll see later in the section about a new definition of sales that it comes with a price. When you imagine these "asshole" salespeople, do you also imagine substance abuse? Bad relationships?

I remember times I was selling to feel better about myself. It wasn't about the client I was selling to; it was about my sense of achievement. And this can be a dangerous place to sell from because you will lack an important key to unlocking sustainable high performance: self-awareness. Even worse, it created a dependency on my sales success. If I had a bad day selling, I would take it personally. This led me to a very yo-yoing emotional state.

The typical solution to this would be to numb myself in the bad days, using distractions, substances, and other external means to bring myself back on my feet. This was a shortcut to bringing myself back to an elevated mood. Yet, it wasn't sustainable, and it didn't make me grow as a person. I'm very grateful to realize that there is a better way, and you'll be learning this, too.

What about Those Scammers?

What about those who take advantage of you? When you get had. Scammed. Lied to. The worst part of being the victim is the embarrassment that comes from it. I know I look back at that time in real estate when it happened to me and can see all the signs now. I remember telling myself things like "How could I be so blind?" and "I can't believe how stupid I was."

I get mad about this part because my shame as a victim, preventing me to speak up, allows the scammers to continue to thrive. I do have to come to terms with the fact that successful scammers are professionals. They understand the human emotional cycles. They have scripts and processes. They can handle objections. It's scary because they can do it while faking empathy. I've come to realize that I can't blame myself for being blind against this force. I hope if you've also been had in the past, you can learn to have an understanding of why it happened and realize it wasn't your fault.

I have now found myself seeking to do what I can to shine a light when things don't happen the way they should. I want to make sure other people don't go through the same problems I did. Even if it's a small infraction, many tools exist to expose this information publicly now. I can leave honest reviews. I can take the time to share my bad experiences and make sure the truth comes out.

Companies need to adapt or rise to the occasion. In fact, this is the most amazing positive effect the internet has had. It didn't kill the need for salespeople. It took away the market for companies and salespeople who controlled the information and manipulated the buyer. And because those people spoke out and demanded more, we are able to see a new breed of companies that are doing the right thing the best way they can.

The internet did come with its own set of challenges and scams as well. There are now platforms allowing anyone to make statements and reach the masses: Facebook, YouTube, TikTok. Everyone can be an "expert" with the newest way to get rich. Fast, easy, no experience necessary, instant millions now. It's scary to witness the most effective methods of marketing being used to promote false promises and fake lifestyles. We have to be vigilant as buyers.

IT GETS BETTER

We took the time to cover some of the worst ideas from sales. Moving forward from here, we will start to make the case for much better sales experiences. This will be true for the buyers and for you, as the seller. When you start to see this possibility, you'll find yourself being much more excited about the sales process in ways you never thought possible before.

ACTION STEPS

1. Self-Assessment

Let's ask a series of power questions to get a little more awareness around your relationship with sales and salespeople. Rate the following questions from 1 to 10, with 1 indicating you strongly disagree and 10 that you strongly agree (5 is neutral).

- Salespeople are looking to help me make the best decision in a buying situation.

- I think salespeople are a key part of making the world a better place.

- I love my product/business/service so much that I sell it as strongly as I can.

- I know exactly who needs my product and why it helps them.

- I keep a pulse on all the latest techniques in sales and marketing and apply them so I can attract and convert more and more people.

2. What's Your Story?

Looking at the ratings you set above for each statement, think of a story you tell yourself that made you rate it as such. Each of these ratings were chosen because of personal experiences or stories from other people. Telling the story here will help you bring into the open the limitations that exist in your sales potential.

CHAPTER 2

THE CASE FOR LIKING SALES

AT THE END OF THE MINDVALLEY EVENT A-FEST, I WAS SITTING in the staff room with my colleague David. Almost everyone knew David at this event. They recognized his voice. And now, they finally met him during the event. Hard to miss this tall Hungarian man with the sharp jawline. He's usually at the back of the seminar room and mingling with the guests during socials. Because he was the one who sold tickets to almost everyone there, they came to see him and thank him personally as well. He was also the man they went to see to buy tickets to the next event or any other product we were selling there. I ask him how the last four days were for him.

"Oh man, it was craaaaazy. I had so many people come up to me who recognized me from the phone calls I made to them, saying,

'Oh! *You're* David! I can't believe you texted me. You called me when it was like 11:00 p.m. You called me so many times. I fucking love you! This event is incredible!'"

I've noticed that people like David absolutely love movement. As a former kickboxing champion in Europe, he was always on the move, on his feet, filled with energy. So he did well in sales, because it's all about moving people along a process to bring an outcome. A good salesperson moves money from the hands of one entity to another in exchange for something. They move people from a negative to a positive frame of mind. I understood David's passion for sales: he was positively twitching with it.

The rest of the team was off enjoying well-earned leisure time as they finished executing a successful event. Since we were the two "sales guys" at A-Fest, our work happened after the event.

"How much money did we close? How many sales did we make?" I asked.

"Dude, we already closed fifty people. That's close to $200,000. I still have over ten. I still need to go find them and get their credit card. How about you?"

I was impressed. We were close to our sales target for the event already. We know 60 percent of the sales happened within twenty-four hours of the event. That window is a critical time to make sure we maximize our sales numbers.

"About three people came to talk to me. I'm going to send a personal email individually to everyone from my Gmail. I want to make sure to land in their inbox. I'll text-message as many as I have their mobile numbers."

This is the time to convert. We just finished the amazing closing party, and everyone is on an emotional high. It's time to make them buy the next event. We were going through the usual processes of reaching everyone in every way we could.

This usual combination of direct sales, marketing, and hustle is our life for the next few days as we try to collect as much money as possible from everyone at the end.

When people came to this event, they left with a shift in their lives like never before. We created new lessons, unforgettable experiences, and connections between people who ran companies that made a massively positive impact on the world. Every time we sold a ticket to A-Fest, we knew that we had just hit the "exponential" button. If the CEO of a company gets a transformation, all their employees would be positively affected. All their customers would also. And all their suppliers/investors. So much value got created when people attended, and partnerships formed between the attendees. New businesses have been created at A-Fest. New charities, too. And even romantic relationships! (Fact: over three wedding proposals have happened and two actual weddings!)

As you read this story, I'm curious to know what ideas went through your head. Did you feel like it was the usual banter you would expect from two salespeople? What judgments did you make of our activities? If I'd shared the story from my design team who were working on the updates to the logo and colors for the next event, would it have the same emotional charge?

A clue for the transformation you need comes from your emotions in that story. If you felt excited, inspired, and wanted to learn more, then you might actually be able to skip this chapter entirely.

If you did see some negative emotion pop up, then please continue, because my goal is, at a minimum, to make a powerful case for you to like sales. Forget selling from love for now. Let's get at least some energy into place to make you like it first.

THE TRUE LENS OF SALES: COMMUNICATION

Last chapter, we talked a lot about the bad sales. Now let's see the world through a new lens.

I hate to use a substitution word to talk about sales because that goes against the point of the book. I will use it once here to bridge the gap and open the possibility of liking sales.

Communication.

Sales is communication with much clearer objectives. And if we start to look at better examples from our current times, we have to study amazing people who are incredible salespeople.

"We choose to go to the moon—not because it is easy, but because it is hard."

Most Americans are familiar with this quote. The rest of the world knows it as well. Imagine the task of getting an entire nation aligned to the goal of spending enormous amounts of money for a program to get humans to land on the moon.

That speech included one key component. The power of setting a vision, a purpose, a declaration of impact that lets people understand the answer to the most important question at the back of their minds: why?

Once people understand the why, people are ready to accept the what and the how. This has been preached during Simon Sinek's famous TED Talk and his book *Start with Why*.[1] It absolutely applies to sales and marketing as well.

"Oh, and one more thing."

Steve Jobs's signature tagline at the end of the annual keynote talk at the Apple events would always get people thinking, "OMG, what crazy new feature is also included?" This is a powerful way to make people take action and get excited about an offer. This one-more-thing keeps people engaged, makes people anticipate a bonus announcement. Since Jobs had done it so many times, it even tapped

---

1   Simon Sinek, "How Great Leaders Inspire Action," TEDx Puget Sound, September 2009, https://www.ted.com/talks/simon_sinek_how_great_leaders_inspire_action.

into people's need for consistency and commitment (see Robert Cialdini's book on influence[2]). As such, they know that last announcement will be a joy—we anticipate it—and they end the presentation with a great hype.

Steve Jobs was a master salesperson. You might think that his most important sales were to the individuals who needed to buy the iPhone or Mac product being launched. He would talk to his entire team inside the company and sell them on the idea that whatever they had created wasn't good enough. He made them believe something more beautiful, more functional, more incredible could be created. People would comply! We have seen the pace of innovation accelerate as a result of this. Apple still has this sales blood in their DNA from the late Steve Jobs.

SALES IS EVERYWHERE

Sales is everywhere, and usually, it's a damn great thing.

You want to get a job? Guess what an interview is? It's you doing a sales pitch. Selling yourself on why you should be hired.

You want to invite people to your dinner party? Guess what you need to prepare? Yep, your invitation is a sales pitch. It could be as simple as a text message saying, "Hey, want to come over this

---

2 Robert Cialdini, *Influence: The Psychology of Persuasion (New York: William Morrow, 1984).*

weekend for dinner?" Or it could be mailing a formal invitation, depending on what kind of dinner we are talking about here.

How about getting that person you are interested in to go on a date with you? Yep, you'll need to either prepare a sales pitch or refine your marketing to be attractive enough to get leads interested in you.

Here is one sales pitch technique used to "close a deal" that you might have heard before: "Will you marry me?"

It's basically the same as saying, "Sign here," which eventually will be a contract, won't it?

As someone who loves sales, I've started to look at all the little things companies and people do to sell better. I'm at Starbucks, and the friendly staff writes my name on the cup. It's personalized now. I feel good coming here to write. And I keep coming back. They have a process that keeps me coming back.

More elaborate than this, I had the chance to go visit a SpaceX rocket launch from the Kennedy Space Center. I'm excited way more about watching the SpaceX launch than the United Launch Alliance (ULA) one. (Sidenote: Have you ever heard of ULA? Do you know the companies in the alliance? They're Boeing and Lockheed Martin.)

Why was I more excited about SpaceX? I knew the experience would sell me really well! They had a livestream from the command center, and they explained what satellite was going up. They gave details about how fascinating it was that the rocket used for this launch was its third time going into space. Cameras were mounted on various parts of the rocket to see all the angles. The countdown timer showed all the expected events on a timeline to set spectators' expectations on everything.

Now why would the engineers "waste" time adding things like cameras, set up a broadcast, and get news anchors to talk about the event? If the goal was just to launch a rocket with less cost and more reliability, this all seems like a waste, doesn't it?

It's absolutely not. It's what gives investors a chance to witness the whole process. Other potential companies now get a launch plus PR from this initiative. The population also gets excited about space exploration again, making sure the government will fund more space programs, increasing budgets. It makes more people, including the best talent, want to work at SpaceX. It makes everything better, at a fraction of the cost compared to the benefits.

And Elon Musk gets it. Look at how Tesla cars are launched, or any other ventures promoted by him. Elon himself is a real-world example of Tony Stark!

This gives you a massive competitive advantage. Sales is an effective form of communication. And the goal is clear. I've made the mistake of thinking that sales wasn't important when doing business with my colleagues. But once again, sales is extremely important in the workplace as well.

Why do companies take time to discuss purpose, mission, values, and so forth? Because every department needs to align, and sales material is required to do so.

Sales is everywhere. And everyone is a salesperson.

We have no choice about it. We live in a world that is all connected. We have relationships with so many people. And sales builds bridges. Nothing to hate about that, right?

HEALING THE EMOTIONAL BLOCKS

What We Learned as Children

Let's get into the practical here. Let's start the process of healing past events that make us resist or hate sales.

What makes us feel safe and loved and what doesn't are mostly formed at a young age. A whole industry of books/courses/events/programs exists to support people continuously dealing with all these scars. What I haven't heard yet, however, is how our childhood experiences affect our confidence in sales as adults. I had some theories that I wanted to bring forward to an expert in the field. Luckily, I was well connected with Shelly Lefkoe of the Lefkoe Institute.

Shelly and her late husband, Morty, have worked over the years with tens of thousands of people who are looking to heal their childhood traumas. Their method, The Lefkoe Method, has been raved about by legends in the field of personal growth as a highly effective treatment.[3]

---

3 The Lefkoe Institute, "Home," Mortylefkoe.com, https://www.mortylefkoe.com/.

During our conversation, I wanted to see if she had worked on clients specifically with sales blocks. Unsurprisingly, this was a common issue they would work on. Even professional salespeople have blocks we all face in the realm of sales. Our subconscious can take over and make us believe things such as *I'm not likable; people won't buy from me. Selling is sleazy. It's not okay to be pushy. If someone doesn't buy from me, I've done something wrong.* This can play in our minds like an annoying whisper in a theater during a movie. It's draining and affects our ability to get up and charge forward to the next sale.

We discussed further, and I highlighted to her two particular events that would be very typical for children in Canada and certainly in many other parts of the world. I wanted to understand if this could be the source of many of the beliefs listed above. On sharing these examples, she confirmed strongly that these need to be investigated and healed.

As children, we are natural salespeople, aren't we? We go up to any stranger to make friends. We want a toy? We get very enthusiastic about it and ask without any resistance. Are we persistent? I'm sure every parent is rolling their eyes. A typical scene would go like this: "Mom/Dad, I saw this new Nintendo and I really, really, really want it. Can we get it? Please. Please, please? [Ten minutes pass] PLLLLLL-LEASE, I really, really want it!!"

Here is what can happen with children's openness to people and their aggressive sales pitches.

First, very quickly, we get reminded not to talk to strangers. The world is not safe.

Is it a surprise that as adults, the idea of prospecting for new clients is one of the biggest struggles for salespeople?

The idea of reaching out to a stranger is terrifying! A new meaning needs to be created here. You are an adult now and talking to strangers is fine. If you find yourself having this natural fear of strangers, this is a belief you really need to investigate and work on.

Second, kids are fearless salespeople but very terrible ones. They don't understand their client or know any techniques on how to close better. They just are annoying, nonstop, persistent, and exhausting salespeople. But you can't hang up the phone or walk away from these little perky sales minions. A scene all too common will happen in their young lives. As a parent, you will snap. (Maybe...probably...nah, *you will*.) And it will sound something like this after ten minutes of annoyance from the kid: "HEY! NO MEANS NO! STOP ASKING."

Can you imagine the meaning created for this child? In this case, the child feels unsafe to ask for what they want. They learn that asking for what you want means your parents won't love you. What you want is not important and isn't worth pursuing. Now, if this has happened with your child, not all is lost. We all lose our temper, and let's face it, kids are annoying, untrained salespeople. As you may have noticed this interaction in your own childhood, it's also important to assume you can learn how this was a trained behavior and overcome it.

Fast-forward to today and imagine being in a sales interaction. How motivated are you to be persistent and follow up with the lead? It's not surprising that the average number of times someone follows up is usually too low to make the sale happen.

Here are some fun statistics:

- Forty-four percent of salespeople give up after one follow-up.

- Ninety-two percent of salespeople give up after no sales on the fourth call. Sixty percent of customers say no four times before saying yes.[4]

People in sales quit too early, thinking, "Oh, if they were really interested, they would get back to me."

Maybe you hesitate. You spend time thinking of when it's best to call. Wait another day. Move on to another task. Weeks go by and you feel like it would be totally awkward to follow up now. Like calling a friend to wish them happy birthday after it passed months ago.

Healing is required. Don't worry, if this seems strange and you are not sure if these issues really affect you, you'll be happy to know that by following the chapters in this book, you'll naturally get to take steps to become a relentless salesperson—in the best way possible.

At this time, I simply want you to be aware of your patterns.

---

4   Ryan Hadfield, "53 Sales Follow-Up Statistics," ZoomInfo, December 6, 2017, https:// blog.zoominfo.com/sales-follow-up-statistics/.

Your First Purchases

It's funny how the image of a used car salesman seems to be prevalent in the idea of a toxic salesperson. In Canada where I grew up, getting your driver's license was truly the ticket to freedom. You then go out there for your first car purchase. It's very likely that you start with a used car. Here we are, excited about getting our freedom, looking at a major purchase, and being completely inexperienced at sales situations.

Your innocence might have been quickly taken away after you dealt with a salesperson who had studied the process of sales and influence.

And if it isn't a car purchase, there are chances that growing up, you've been had in your first major purchases, leaving you very hesitant and resistant to everything that brings back that negative experience.

And if it wasn't your own direct negative experience going through this, you might have heard negative stories from a friend or relative.

Our minds will always notice and remember the dangers first. We were programmed that way since prehistoric times. It was much more important to remember the poisonous berries than to remember the really tasty ones, because our survival was at stake.

This leaves you with all those vivid impressions from the negative sales experiences, while the many times you had good or great sales interactions go unnoticed.

This wouldn't be a big deal if it wasn't for the effect this has on you today. Every time you come to the point of selling, you find yourself resistant. You'd rather do "creative work" or anything else. More often than not, what is needed to move the needle is, in fact, going out there and selling. Why would you want to step into the shoes of that person who wronged you, doing what they did? Feeling like you'll become that salesperson who will "wrong" your client, as you remember vividly?

It's like climbing a mountain with a bungee cord attached to the base. It slows you down, uses more energy, and will ultimately prevent you from going the distance.

That salesperson probably doesn't remember you. They won't know the pain they caused. Only you hold on to that. It's time to let it go. You will never know what was happening in their lives that made them do this to you. They could be evil, but most likely, they didn't know better. They had their own priorities and thought that this was the only way to make a sale happen. Yet, as you'll learn through this book, they also have a price to pay when they sell this way. As for you, you'll learn to heal this, let it go, and move on. Sales has much more positive moments than negative. Focus on this. You'll be one of the people who creates these beautiful, positive moments for people.

CHOOSING BETTER ROLE MODELS

I'd always have a little fun when I'd ask everyone about who their idols were. When I ask this question, there are always a few obvious famous people that come up. Oprah, Steve Jobs, Elon Musk, Arianna Huffington, and so forth. The answer to that question usually comes very quickly.

The follow-up question usually leaves people thinking a little more.

"For the role model you selected, do you think they are a salesperson?"

A pause.

See, people who want to solve big problems in the world will need to sell their ideas—to the masses. This is no small task. If you want to be motivated to like sales, remember that everyone you look up to has done a great job of selling themselves.

Yet, I want to open up one possibility. The idea of sales done in a pushy, manipulative way to be effective is only a portion of the story. Most people who are in sales successfully are very caring and confident and build long-term relationships. And this is how you can open yourself up to realize that by focusing on only the bad, you limit yourself on the potential impact you could make when this is no longer a block in your life.

It's quite interesting to also note that most people in CEO positions in the world have a sales and marketing background. It truly is a skill that, once mastered, can help you rise in any field to shake the world.

SELLING HAS EVOLVED

When the internet was emerging and growing, there was much talk about the decline of the salesperson. People were celebrating that fact, again, because there was little to no awareness of all the good that is done by salespeople. What did happen was that consumers now had access to so much more information than ever before. In the past, when information had been scarce, the salespeople controlled this information. That doesn't feel right. When the person controlling the information is incentivized to take a certain action, it's a recipe for disaster. Thank the internet for this new world of data abundance.

Yet, now we have a new problem. There is too much of it. And it becomes so hard to make decisions because of the overload. Plus, let's not forget the surge in scams, fake news, and information, as well as social media newsfeeds that seem to manipulate our perspectives.

Salespeople now have come to the rescue, yet their roles have essentially changed.

Although they used to be gatekeepers of information, they're now educators and dealing with reputation management.

Clients have become much more aware, and it's forced many companies to evolve. When you buy something, you've been trained to be able to see reviews all over the place. Amazon has thousands of reviews per product, and cars everywhere are independently reviewed. Even employers are reviewed on platforms like Glassdoor.

People are also looking to buy from companies who have taken the time to explain the why of their existence. The rise of the conscious consumer is a powerful trend and included many people with some of the highest disposable income. If you hold this book in your hands, you'll be one of the beneficiaries of this trend. You are also going to play a part in it yourself. Once you are done with this book, you'll also be empowered as an even more selective and caring employee, buyer, and everyday human being.

The case for caring is key, and we play the part of buying and selling in our everyday lives, all the time.

ACTION STEPS

1. Think of any bad sales experience you had. Make a list of ways you grew stronger/better from those events. Tell the story from a position of power, not victimization.

2. Think of the things in your life that you absolutely enjoyed buying and owning.

3. Make a list of your role models. See what makes them a salesperson.

4. Write down a declaration on a page with the following: "I am a salesperson." Follow up with a list of memorable achievements in your life as a result of you selling (getting that job, doing a great presentation, finding a partner, getting your kids to listen, direct sales experience, etc.).

CHAPTER 3

A NEW DEFINITION OF SALES

I REMEMBER READING THE DICTIONARY DEFINITION OF SELLING, and it was quite dry:

> *Selling: the act of giving or handing over (something) in exchange for money.*

Here is a new definition I'd want you to consider as a reader of this book:

> *Selling: an energy exchange between two conscious beings.*

As two individuals connect, communicate, and agree (or disagree), a sale is made. Through these processes, there is an exchange, a movement, a change that occurs. Yet, the most important part of the formula is the energy.

I choose the word "energy" deliberately because we can soon realize that everything can be traced back to energy at its source. Let's look at the common elements in a sales transaction and see how they work back to energy.

WHAT IS ENERGY IN THE CONTEXT OF SALES?

Money

Let's start with the obvious one. We need to further break down money into what it truly is, because so many people have beliefs, stories, and limitations when it comes to money. A common one is that "money is the root of all evil." This sounds blasphemous to me.

Let's use some simple examples here. Where does the money come from? What is it? How did *you* get it? If you are working in a career, then you'll know that the money is the result of putting time and effort into your work. Your labor is rewarded with money. Or as an entrepreneur, your profits from your activities, when done right, will bring in money.

Money is nothing more than stored energy. Can you imagine the time when bartering was happening? Let's say you were an egg farmer, and all you could offer others was eggs. If you want anything in your community, you better have people interested in buying eggs. Otherwise, you couldn't get anything. (God forbid you were in a vegan community. Then you'd be in serious trouble.) Our entire economy around money has been a process of creating more freedom by allowing people to store energy. The fruits of our labor can now be captured, saved, invested, used, and more. It's the greatest innovation ever. To label it as "evil" doesn't do any good.

So if we realize money is stored energy, we know it's a critical part of the energy exchange.

Products/Services

How was your product or service created? Did it require raw materials? Manufacturing? Did people work in that factory? Or if it's a service, did you need to prepare the service delivery? Did you have processes that bring value to people?

All products and services are also energy. They are energetic creations as a result of labor, raw materials, and refinement. A chair you sit on can be made from wood, cut from trees by people. Refined and assembled, other materials were added. It's absolutely fascinating if you look at all the stuff we have in our lives and track back how it was created. We are in such an age of abundance that we have lost connection with awareness of the supply chain. Imagine if we had full visibility and appreciation of what goes into the process of creating a plastic bag. We scoff at a five-cents charge for the bag at the store.

Once again, products and services are energetic creations. Energy was extracted from raw materials and put into creation.

Here's a note about a kind of "product" that can be sold: ideas. In a boardroom, everyone is trying to sell why their idea is so important and should be prioritized. If you want to make plans with your partner, you need to sell it to them. Kids need to eat their veggies. Think of ideas as an energy exchange as well. When you "sell" someone else to follow your plan, you've changed the course of action. Now time and energy will be used to make this idea a reality.

Time

Time is money. Some people don't like that quote. It can sound too aggressive because again, our ideas around money are so charged. But first, let's correct one common misconception around the phrase.

If time = money, and money = stored energy, then does time = stored energy?

No. Time is not stored energy. The real difference is that time is an instantly expiring energy source. If not used the moment it's available, it is no longer available. And this can be a source of great fear for some. That's why many state that time is more valuable than money. It's our most important resource.

I remember a period in my life when I was so paranoid of the fleeting nature of time that any moment I wasn't using to maximize output with my time, I felt disappointed and depressed. There is much to learn about how we want to best use our time. Entire books have been dedicated to the subject.

What I want you to stay aware of is that time can be a big factor in a sales transaction. The time it takes for the sale to happen. The time it takes for people to use the product or service. The time it takes to create and deliver the products/services. Time becomes a major item of optimization. You'll be able to see new opportunities to serve better, cut costs, and scale when you truly appreciate the value of time in every transaction.

Time = active energy.

Risk

We are all creatures who practice the art of risk management, consciously or not. Every time you propose a sale, people automatically need to evaluate the risks of making versus not making the decision to exchange. Minimizing this risk is one of the key ways to make sales happen. Are the promises of what this product/service will do true? Am I getting a good deal? Are there other options? What if it breaks? What if it doesn't work? What if my friends judge me for it? What if my spouse feels left out of the decision-making process? The list goes on. Risk is the silent killer of an energy exchange. You'll learn how to minimize these risks so the transaction can move forward.

There is a final piece to this formula that most people forget about: emotions. And you'll learn very quickly how understanding this will make or break your sales career.

THE FOUR EMOTIONS IN THE SALES PROCESS THAT ARE HOLDING YOU BACK

When you make a transaction, emotions are the hidden variables at play. And they're on both sides of the equation. The buyer will be left with a feeling after the transaction, and so will the seller.

There are four levels to these emotions. Each will create an effect that is different from the others. Let's break them down.

1. Shame-Guilt Blockages

The mind can be a tricky thing while in the middle of a crisis. I found myself sitting at a pizza shop outside the city with my dad. I had called him earlier that day asking for help. I'd gone a few weeks feeling I was trapped in a cage. I was going crazy. I had imagined every worst-case scenario for every client I sold property to. I ran ideas on how they would lose all their money, they would think I manipulated them, lied to them, and ultimately betrayed them. I was going around in circles trying to ensure that I did everything as perfect as possible. Yet, even this was not good enough. As the information I knew about real estate was being challenged, I felt like I was stuck.

My dad asked me what was wrong, and I couldn't explain. All that came out was a sort of confused gibberish. "Everything is wrong. I don't know what I'm doing. The transaction process was done wrong. The business structures are confusing. I don't know if they will be hit with double tax. I'm going crazy and I can't work."

I was in my early twenties and feeling completely overwhelmed by the situation I was in. I should have been happy. I have lots of sales! Over half a million dollars' worth. I was one of the most successful students of the real estate investor education program with my two partners, who were also my best friends. They both were trying to comfort me, saying, "Relax. We are going to fix this. We are going to make it good for everyone." Yet, it seemed impossible in my mind that a solution existed.

My dad wasn't very good with emotions. He was more of an "everything is fine all the time" kind of man, keeping to himself and showing strength. Yet in this moment, he had a level of understanding I didn't expect.

"Jason, you aren't weak. You aren't doing anything wrong. But there is something happening in your mind, and you simply need to talk to a doctor. I've been through stressful times, and I've had to get mental health professionals to support me. So please, tomorrow, you go see our local doctor who might prescribe something, or maybe not. But you'll be able to get help, because right now, you are not yourself."

Depression was really weird for me. It was caused by stress. And it seems so strange when I think of it in hindsight. After that meeting where it seemed my mind simply wanted to have actionable steps to move forward, making that appointment was a huge step. After this was settled, he extracted from me a list of problems I was feeling paralyzed by.

First one: the real estate transaction flow.

His simple question in response to this was, "Who is a person that could get you the answer? A title agent?"

Yes. I scheduled a call to contact Tony Singleton, my title agent who would help me through getting those answers. One less burden.

And one by one, we identified all the issues and set up one action item for each.

Relief followed. I got the help from the doctor. I took antidepressants for a short while. It supported me as I ensured every client I sold to was taken care of to the best of my abilities, even if that wasn't perfect.

As I think back on that dark time, it reveals a warning of what happens when you sell with shame-guilt blockages. I had deep fears of disappointing clients. I had an expectation of doing everything right, all the time. Any mistake would be a failure of my character.

In this example, I had made many sales while I was under the illusion that everything was okay; ignoring warning signs along the way, I charged forward in this new business venture. Yet in most cases for shame-guilt blockages, the same never happens. I hesitate, I get distracted, I make excuses. It really is a place where the block itself seems insurmountable.

To clear these emotions, there is some major work we need to do. If not, we fall short of our goals and self-sabotage, both personally and in business. Under these conditions, sales will not bring abundance. It will not serve the world. There is very little to no good that will come of it. It will be a fight in your mind every time. You will feel worse and worse as you continue. You will soon be choosing ways to distract or numb yourself to avoid facing the reality. Trust me, I've been there, and it's been some of the lowest points in my life. I felt like a fraud because, in fact, I was. To myself.

Good news is, there is much we can do about it and a few options to look into for making this better.

The key theme to move out of these emotions is clearing them. Shame, guilt, and grief are all emotions to process and let go. See if these emotions only affect your work or every part of your life. If it's only work, the cause of shame, guilt, and grief might only be circumstantial to your job.

Just make sure you spend some time thinking and seeing how your views and beliefs on sales could be a source of the guilt and shame. I trust that the work we did in the first chapters has already started to shift your view to help with this.

If like me, you are concerned with your mental health (often with the feedback of people who love you), seeking medical help is always encouraged and supported. I know I was very grateful I did. So do check in with yourself and see if this needs further investigation.

I will say that shame-guilt blockages are not all negative. They can serve as useful allies for your consciousness. An example would be when you find yourself asking for too much money for a subquality product/service. This is a clue that this needs to change. You can recognize it as an opportunity to do better. Regardless of the source of the blockages, powerful information is being presented to you to investigate and transcend.

2. The Fear-Pride Paradox

This next set of emotions is really tricky. When you operate from a position of fear and pride, you need to be personally validated by the sale at a deep level. Yes, maybe you'll move deals forward quickly. Yet, you are operating in a self-serving world.

Let me tell you another story about how I fell into this problem.

I was on the phone with a Canadian man who wanted to start investing in real estate in the United States. Makes sense, since I was working for the company who sold me the coaching program one year back. I had helped to rebuild this program for Canadians, and now here I was, selling it to other people.

My job was to take away the uncertainty and close the sale. Yet, something was different in this interaction: Josh was concerned about his criminal record.

This means he could not step on US soil. It's indeed a little risky to own real estate in a country you can't enter. But at that time, my job was simple: close the sale.

I followed my usual scripts. I told him how the entire program was built to support people to buy the properties "sight unseen." I told him how I've bought and sold properties from Canada. I assured him that he especially should buy the program, given his situation. I could sense his apprehension, so I pushed it even further. The call started with him saying, "I'm sorry, there is no way I can do this, given my situation." Now after a few minutes on the phone, he was telling me, "Damn it! I wasn't ready to buy this, but you make lots of good points...I need to think about it."

And then, in my most confident way, inspired by all the sales movies, I pushed one more time for the close.

"Listen, if you simply 'think' about doing real estate, don't do it," I pressed him. "When a good deal comes by and you stop and think, I move and buy. When opportunity knocks, I'm at the door with flowers. And this is what we will teach you, too. I'm offering you the best deal on this coaching and I'm knocking loudly so you can hear. I even brought the flowers myself so you are ready. I just need you to take a small step and put down the deposit to kick this off. Are you ready to make serious money in the US? Because we are serious about making sure you get there."

Josh was silent. I was, too. The few seconds after I delivered what I felt was an Oscar-winning speech felt like hours. (Sales tip: when making a pitch with an attempt to close, it's always best to just sit in the silence. Nothing more needs to be said. You have to wait for the response.) Finally, Josh opens his mouth.

"Okay, I'm in! Let me put together the funds and send the wire this afternoon!"

Pause.

Sales here are often done without an understanding of the impact of what you do. If you have been on the buying side of the equation, you've probably felt a sense of neediness from the seller. They need to make this sale happen. They come across as pushy and inauthentic. They're not bad people. More often than not, it's a problem of lacking self-awareness.

If you're a seller with this problem, like I was with Josh, then you feel scarcity in your life (fear), so you try to fix it by pushing for more sales. You want to be a better salesperson, or at least recognized as one (desire). So you work harder, push harder, and feel frustrated when you don't hit your targets. You see people who aren't buying right now as time wasters (anger). You get frustrated with how they don't get it. You sell because you want to show to everyone around you and yourself how amazing you are at selling (pride).

Have you ever listened to the scandals and scams that people got sold into and thought, "Wow, how did that happen?" This is it. People accidentally (or intentionally) nurture the buyer's inexperience or unpreparedness and end up losing all their savings. If you've seen *The Wolf of Wall Street*, this is exactly what's at play. Selling at this level is a zero-sum game. There are takers and losers.

When I was selling to Josh, I had something to prove. I was looking to express how awesome I was in sales. My ego was more important to me than the actual outcome for the client. It was the sales application of hubris. And this type of pride, in combination with the fear of not selling, is extremely dangerous. It can make you hyperfixate on all the tricks in the book in hopes of increasing your performance. And you will. But it comes at a cost.

Josh could move forward with the program, yet a big portion of the value came from actually going to the United States, which he couldn't with his criminal record.

Josh may have had his own priorities and goals, yet, with the beautiful stories and promises I made, felt that it was better to move forward with my offer. But I offered no guarantee, and what I said was not an accurate picture of what he would face. It was quite embellished.

What must not be forgotten is that as a seller, you do have a responsibility for every sale. This is why if you sell without integrity—if you don't assume that responsibility—it will still be felt. I know, for me, I didn't feel it until later when I had a chance to slow down and look back at my sales methods and see where I had fallen short. In the midst of selling from this level, you keep yourself busy, distracted, and moving. Think of it as a defense mechanism that doesn't want to face the negatives of your actions.

How do you get out? As I mentioned earlier, this is really an exercise in self-awareness. If you recognize yourself in this category, you need to search within and see if the transactions you are making are really for the benefit of the person beyond yourself. Do you take the time to slow down? Do you think back on everyone you sold to in the last year? What emotions come up? Do you feel good? Bad? Indifferent? Take notice. Later in the book, we will cover how to sell with love more consistently. Tools there will help you gut check how to do better. For now, just be aware.

I know I started my journey here. Awareness will either come through proactive learning or possibly a swift slap in the face if you don't take action. I know in my case, I got lucky and shifted out before it got too bad.

3. Rational Sabotage

What is rational sabotage? It's the realm of sales limbo. Sometimes salespeople focus too much on the rational things people are looking for in products or services.

You take the time to explain fully all the features and benefits of a product, and the client seems bored or confused and doesn't buy.

You don't use any of the sales tactics the "other" people use and explain things your way to the customer, and they still buy from the competitor who had a "100 percent money-back guarantee."

You explain to the customer that you will be taking great care of them like family, and they seem scared of your neediness and shop elsewhere.

What breaks my heart about selling from this place is that my intentions always seem to be from a "good" place. I'm trying to show more care and empathy toward the buyer. I'm trying to care more by giving more information. Unfortunately, this usually backfires. Buyers can be left with having to do more work to decide among the flood of information available. In the spirit of trying to care more, we actually do not become helpful. We create more confusion.

Remember Microsoft Zune? Probably not. It was a music player launched in 2006. It had more features than the iPod at the time. Microsoft had done everything to make a better product. More songs could fit in it. It was faster. All of the rational benefits you could throw into the machine at the time were there. Yet, it was a massive failure when it launched.

With rational sabotage, sales don't happen as much, even though data would suggest it shouldn't be this way. I've had times where I butt my head against the wall thinking this was support to work, and it failed.

Why is that? When you operate from this level, you might not realize the hidden block. Giving lots of information, data, and rational reasons to buy isn't about taking responsibility for the sale. Rather, it's about giving so much overwhelming information to the buyer that you try to put the responsibility on them. They don't want it, and that's why the sales fail.

It's also about forgetting one critical element about selling: you need to sell while speaking a language the buyer responds to, not the language that *you* respond to.

The shame-guilt blockages were about running away from responsibility. The fear-pride paradox was about not caring about responsibility. Rational sabotage is about trying to give responsibility to the buyer.

Now, what would bring you, a seller, to the stage of rational sabotage? This next level is one that I stepped into at times when I wanted to do "better" than selling with pride.

Every time I'm here, there are two emotional words that come to mind: "neediness" and "insecurity."

I'd get on the phone with people. I'd tell them not to decide right now. I'd share with them lots of PDFs, links, and other information related to the purchase. I'd use phrases like "It's up to you" and "Let me know when you are ready."

If they decide yes, good. If they decide no, good. It's out of my control. It's not my responsibility.

Let me give you another example. Once, while running a program called Mindvalley Mentoring, my team decided to test new amenities for the people in this membership in order to keep them subscribed. The sale here wasn't focused on collecting money. It was about giving more value to existing members. We wanted to minimize the churn rate—this is the number of people who cancel their membership. By doing this event, I wanted to deliver something they would all enjoy.

I thought, *What if I do live training and get people to experience a mastermind online?* This training would be a networking-style event where structure is provided to solve specific business or personal issues.

The plan was simple. I'd set up a place where I could deliver this live training. And toward the end of the session, I would break the attendees into groups of five to discuss further and solve problems in their lives and business. I was excited to deliver this.

It was time to promote this event to our members. I wrote a message to everyone on the community forum. "Hey, everyone! If you are looking to gain new insights and perspective while getting a chance to connect with the community, join me for a live training plus mastermind, and you'll have fun and gain so much from it!"

We had done a survey a couple of weeks before, and these were the three things they wanted more in the tribe: live interaction, more community, more content. Pretty straightforward, right?

As we sent out the invitation sharing this, I went live on the call and waited for people to join. With over ten thousand members, I was expecting to see the limit of one hundred people hit in minutes and having to tell people, "Wow, this was so great. You'll need to register in advance as these sessions sell out!"

Five minutes past the scheduled start time, the first client logged in.

And over the course of the next sixty minutes, we had a total of two more people join. They all received a private coaching session with me.

Hmm, I missed the mark here. I was able to give massive value to the people who showed up, but where was everybody else?

This is the trap of selling to the mind. It can work, but it can also be the source of frustration when you see it fail to meet expectations. Good news is that you'll never feel like you cheated yourself or the person you are selling to. As a matter of fact, this is the level I found myself on after doing self-work and questioning the moments I sold with pride.

I wanted to do better. I chose to do only certain methods of selling and avoid the ones that felt too "manipulative." I positioned it in my mind as "me versus them" and became a martyr of my own selling methods. Results didn't show, yet I was one of the "good" guys.

This was not the right way to go at it. It should not have been about what was comfortable for me to sell. Instead, it's about what is valuable to the buyer. When you answer that question, then you find the best ways to speak their language.

The good news is that moving beyond this isn't a big leap. It's much simpler than you think.

Heads-Up to My Techie and Creative Friends

I've noticed a large portion of my colleagues, especially the creatives and tech specialists, find rational sabotage of selling to be a default position. Heck, even I find myself there when I try to push through complex software into the company and don't take the time to understand the needs and impact to all affected people. Like bringing in an advanced customer relationship management software (CRM) into the company sales team.

I fully understood CRM's capabilities. And I just told people about all the amazing features. I recorded videos showing them why I thought it was so important to bring it into the company. In my head, I could see how this would revolutionize our sales efficiency.

Yet, everyone was confused. It looked like more work for everyone. And it didn't align with company priorities. I was oblivious to all of this and was left with having everyone resisting the technology and even being suspicious of my overenthusiasm. (I think some people even thought I was getting a commission from that company.)

And you'd think I would have learned my lesson after the first try. Another time, I did it again within my father's swimming pool company. Yet for this, it was even worse. I didn't sell to the team at all. I made the decision on my own and didn't include the users in the process. In an effort to cut corners and "show it in action" instead of selling it properly, I pushed it through as it was "rationally" going to be awesome and everyone would love it.

Everyone felt like they weren't included in the decision-making process. This made them resist it, and in the end, it didn't reach the potential it could have had. As I mentioned at the beginning of this section, rational sabotage usually starts with great intentions. Yet, it forgets to bring into focus one of the most important pieces of the puzzle: serving the buyer.

4. Love

When a person is motivated by love, joy, peace, and enlightenment, there is very little that can stop them from getting into the right state and taking massive action to deliver something truly amazing in their field.

I sometimes find people operating from this level in the most random of places. Coming back from a trip to see a SpaceX rocket launch in Florida, I knew I had a three-hour drive to Miami where I lived. I needed some food, and the only place available at the time was a Subway before the entrance to the highway. Between that, Burger King, and Checkers, I did the best I could with the cards I was dealt.

The moment I walked into this store, Jane (let's call her Jane; I wish I remembered her name) was behind the counter with a giant smile and the enthusiasm you'd only see from a child explaining to you how their new toy works. She greeted me saying, "Welcome! Oh my god, did you just go see the rocket launch? How was it? I'm glad you're here. All the bread is fresh, and I can get you anything you like."

I couldn't help but notice my level of enthusiasm matched hers. I ordered the tuna sub and she casually suggested, "Listen, you can do a double tuna or a deluxe version for a little more of the tuna. But let's be honest here, you probably have a long road ahead, and I've never heard anyone say they regretted getting the double tuna."

I bought double tuna. Duh.

Throughout the whole time making the sub, she was vibrant and joyful. I left a major tip at the end. I don't think I had ever tipped at Subway before. Yet after seeing this, I felt amazing! The sub was the best sandwich on the planet. I swear! She was enjoying her work so much because that was the choice she had made.

Here lies a clue in energy exchanges. This is why selling at this level is beyond anything you can measure in sales. This is the secret sauce to getting yourself to break through sales records.

When you know that what you offer is going to be so much more than what you ask in return, you start selling from a place of love.

Jane felt that for the price of the sub I wanted, I was about to get the most amazing food to support me on the road home. Her upsell: she knew that I had a big appetite. Walking away without this premium upgrade, I'd be missing out on incredible value.

She didn't need to fake her enthusiasm. If she had, the message would be tainted. When it comes from a place of authenticity, people know it, and you know it. The buyer and seller are both left with an amazing feeling of seeing the transaction happen.

That's how you start selling with zero resistance.

Think about how Tesla launched their cars. I remember the launch event for the Model 3 and the Cybertruck. It was a big show! And the Model 3 had over 500,000 preorders! That's almost $15 *billion* in presales for a car that was going to be ready in a few years. And for the Cybertruck: by the end of summer 2021, there were over 1.25 million preorders for this model, resulting in $79 billion in potential sales revenue.[5]

How did they do it? Let's look at the Cybertruck example. To introduce that launch event, a virtual hologram woman described the problems with gas-powered vehicles. Then Elon Musk came to the stage surrounded by a grand light show that could have been from a rock concert. Everything was designed to make an impression on the client in mind: truck buyers. The tests that followed demonstrated the superior "toughness" of the Cybertruck. Some elements didn't go perfectly (slides were off, the glass of the truck broke during the demo, and Elon's style was awkward), but overall, it worked. Because at the root of the sales methods, it was done in an authentic way, with a great product, and sold with a focus on

---

5   Dan Mihalascu, "Tesla Now Has More than 1.25 Million Pre-Orders for the Cybertruck," InsideEVs, August 3, 2021, https://insideevs.com/news/524156/tesla-cybertruck-preorders-exceed-1250000/.

making an impact. Of course, these all communicated the company vision in the best way for the clients to understand. Everyone behind this successful event executed it flawlessly: Tesla was not holding back. That's what selling with love looks like. It's the beautiful execution of a sales and marketing event to move a product that truly makes a difference.

There is so much love in everything that is promoted by Tesla. They are driven by a mission to get people to switch over to electric cars and save the planet. Effortless and exciting sales are within your grasp when you understand how to sell with love.

By contrast, I was in the gym the other day where I dragged my friend for a free trial. At the end of the strenuous training, the lead coach tried to sign him up to the gym. I noticed he was using sales tactics that were shaming my friend into making a commitment. The language used included things like "If you can't commit today, you probably don't commit to much in your life" and "Come on, I've gone out of my way to make a deal for you. You should sign up now."

I could feel the resistance in my friend, and I could also see the lack of integrity from the coach. He was motivated to close a sale based on a transactional motivator.

When you come from love, you'll do what it takes to make the sale, knowing that what you are offering is so much more than what you ask in return. *That's* how to go at it from a place of love. You won't need to shame people into deciding.

Going back to Josh who was on the fence about buying that real estate program. It's strange to say now that I'm very glad he didn't buy the program. Although he did say yes on the call, he never followed with the money and finally told me, "I can't do it. I'm sorry." I had used the shame-and-guilt projection technique that left him feeling uninspired to take action. It could have worked, yet it would not have been a loving sale. It would have been an example of the fear-pride paradox: my blind pride in selling would have left the buyer making a decision that I knew, deep down, was not a great decision for him.

This is a problem in the clarity of selling: How much is your product worth to the buyer? Is the value greater than what you ask for in return?

We need to get clear on how to assess value. Making arbitrary assumptions on the value of your product for the buyer is one of the biggest mistakes that prevents people from selling great products to good people. The next chapter will give you the formula that will accurately gauge this customer value.

ACTION STEPS

1. Think about the last three products you bought. Can you identify what was the energy level of the salesperson?

2. The next time you are about to purchase something, try to notice what energy level the person is selling from.

3. When you sell, do you notice your default energy level?

4. For now, don't try to force yourself into a different level. Part 2 of this book will be more prescriptive. Instead, focus on being aware of the energy exchange in every transaction in your daily life.

CHAPTER 4

THE UNDERSTANDING
OF VALUE

IF YOU HAVEN'T NOTICED ALREADY, WE STARTED THIS WHOLE BOOK
dealing with the issues that plague those at the lower levels of emotions. We worked our way up from shame-guilt blockages and the
fear-pride paradox, dealing with the resistance and unlocking the potential. Before we transition to selling from love, we need to first speak
to the concerns that come from rational sabotage.

I am often the one who finds himself at this level. I let myself be affected
by the mental chatter that takes me away from selling from a place of
love and drags me into a place of factual justification. When you end up
in this place, you'll find yourself surprised by how slow the movement of
sales becomes, even if things make sense in your rational mind.

Understanding value is critical here. There are many types of values
involved in the transaction: Your own perception. The perception of

the buyer. The "real" or "objective" value. You'll start putting your mind at ease when you know you are doing the right thing. Once the mind is convinced, you'll have space for the heart to open up, and that's where the abundance lies.

SELL THE VALUE, NOT THE COST

I can't help but think about a time before I joined Mindvalley, when the organization had a program called Zentrepreneur. Members of the program would get to enjoy a live event in a beautiful location such as Costa Rica or the Dominican Republic once a year. During this event, you would have the top speakers in the fields of online marketing, e-commerce, and course creation. They would share their ideas from the stage and mingle with members the whole time.

For the rest of the year, people were kept connected, getting answers to any questions they had. Mindvalley would share their top results from tests they would do to increase sales, create more successful results for clients, and help them build a business with less stress, more impact, and of course, more profit.

For members, they had huge benefits. Most of them found themselves making hundreds of thousands a year. A few were already making millions and looking at a new set of challenges as they moved from one to ten million, and these new arrivals could get answers from people who had just walked the same journey. It was a beautiful concept of a mastermind. To join, you had to apply and be selected. This exclusivity kept a high level of "quality" among the members.

I was aware of this program before I worked for Mindvalley. As I worked in real estate at the time, it appeared to be an amazing opportunity, and we wanted to apply. Yet, we assumed it was too difficult to get in. We estimated this mastermind must have cost around $30,000–$40,000.

Fast-forward one year to my first few weeks in Mindvalley. I was quickly promoted to run the entrepreneurship division. This meant I was going to be in charge of Zentrepreneur. I couldn't believe it! In the transition meeting, my outgoing colleague explained all the products and their price points.

"As for Zentrepreneur, it costs $2,000," they said.

When I explained how I assumed it to be more than twenty times that price, I observed something interesting. My colleague told me this could never be done, as the cost to put together this program had been nowhere near that price, so they couldn't justify that price point. That was when I shared with them my honest opinion that opened this book:

"I can't believe how selfish you are in charging them so little for this program!"

When you price your product according to your costs, this means that you have not taken the time to understand the value you provide to your clients. If you ask me, it's a little lazy. It feels more comfortable to simply say, "Let's add 10–20 percent profit margin on the cost and sell it at that price."

When you price too low, you could fail to maximize impact. You might limit the budget available to acquire more clients. You might not have explored the full-range value you can provide with product changes that are tailored to the needs of the client even more than the original program.

The first thing I did when I started running the program was raise the price to $5,000–$7,000. I had done research on alternatives, gotten to understand what the client was looking for, and seen what could be put together to sell it as such. I even changed the entire sales process to be more personal and consultative as opposed to automated, as our target clients were looking for this kind of concierge experience. Finally, I created a new product line called Zentrepreneur for Startups. This low-price subscription was for an entirely new client base that aspired to join the bigger program. One year into running the department, I created the single most profitable division of Mindvalley. The finance team couldn't believe it, as it was being run by an extremely small team. Yet, we were clear on one thing: we focused on giving value. And we happened to have some of the happiest clients, too.

This is what happens when you stop being focused on your cost. Doing so is centered on your limited perspective. It's lazy, and it's inefficient.

If you are in a good market where you can afford margins, competition is low, and buyers are abundant, you can get away with pricing a product according to your costs rather than its value. The good market floats all sellers. On the flip side, if you are in a market filled with competitors where you are being commoditized (meaning, people see no difference between products aside from price, so everyone competes only by lowering the price), you would be in trouble very quickly.

What's a better strategy overall? You keep focused on the needs of the buyer. You stay open-minded toward problem solving and keep flexible on what you offer. Don't compete with those other companies on the same low-priced product. Upgrade to a more effective one. Then its value justifies the higher price, and the buyer is happier, too.

The buyer doesn't care about your costs. They care about getting a good deal on something that solves their problems.

HOW DO WE SELL VALUE?

Now, why did I think it was worth $30,000–$40,000 to join a mastermind? Looking at the problems in the business I was working in and the solutions this mastermind would provide, it would have generated hundreds of thousands in additional revenue for the member. And that's why it's so important to accurately value the problems you solve for the buyer.

Value is a funny number because it's different for every buyer. If another business owner had just been starting out with barely six figures in revenue, that price would've made no sense for them. The truth is that you cannot truly know the exact value each person gets from your offer. But you can get real close. You can study them. And you can take a bold chance.

Value-based selling is buyer focused. You take the time to study what problems they have in their lives. Then you start to estimate how much pain this causes and how valuable it would be for them to not have that problem.

In a business-to-business (B2B) setting, you would zero in on:

- What costs can you save them?

- What risks can you lower?

- What activities can you make happen more quickly?

- What processes can you make easier?

- What opportunities can you help them capture?

Quantifying value in these settings usually becomes much more concrete. Of course, even if you get very clear on the value, sometimes it doesn't magically result in a sale. But you'll at least have confidence in the success of the transaction once it's done.

For a business-to-consumer (B2C) transaction, you'll actually have the exact list as above. The only difference is that you'll have a much bigger focus on your buyer's emotions.

Once you start understanding the value people get from buying, you'll have a much better idea on how to price accordingly, maximize the number of potential buyers at a price point, and be profitable in the process.

THE TWO KINDS OF VALUES
FOR THE BUYER

Now, I want you to keep in mind that value can actually be split into two different types: *real value* and *perceived value*. Don't be alarmed: this is actually very simple to understand and powerful to know.

Until an individual purchases what you offer, uses it, and theoretically reports back to you the exact value they received, even they don't know the real value of the product. The perceived value is all they know. Understanding the difference between the real value and perceived value in a transaction is incredibly important to sell more effectively.

Perceived Value = The Most They Will Pay for a Product

Perceived value is what the buyer believes this purchase will potentially offer them. It is, in fact, purely motivated by expectations. When you are considering buying a product or service, this is really what will influence the decision to say yes. If the perceived value is higher than the price, then it's a good deal in the mind of the buyer.

Let's take, for example, the time I was around Walt Disney World in Orlando (Animal Kingdom, to be more precise). I had a problem. It's a terrible problem to have at a theme park (worse at a Disney one): I got hungry. Lo and behold, I saw a sign for a giant pretzel. Given how hungry I was, I went to get one. I got to the cash register, and it was seven dollars. I still bought it.

Why did I buy it? I was thinking, *This pretzel is the best I'll get to maximize my hunger satisfaction.* Given few alternatives, it looked like the perceived value was over seven dollars. Transaction complete.

Funny example, yet it illustrates the point. I felt what was being sold would satisfy a need more than any other options at that moment. I didn't ask how much it cost them to make the pretzel.

How is perceived value determined? As mentioned earlier, it always depends on the buyer, their needs, their problems, and how important it is for them to solve those problems. As the seller, there is much you can do to influence this value. That's the role of marketing and sales.

If you use marketing wisely, it'll do a great job of making sure people are aware. Aware of your existence. Aware of the problems. Aware of the solutions. Aware of the benefits, features, and more.

You, the salesperson, will do your best to make sure your client feels like you understand their core needs. Then you can solve their problems when they buy your product.

Real Value = The Actual Value of the Purchase

At this point, I'm eating this pretzel and realize that it's unhealthy and a little dry and I'm still hungry. I regret buying it, and I feel a little cheated in the process. I can't believe I had to pay seven dollars for this!

This is when the real value comes into play.

The difference between a happy customer and a sad one is how the real value is reflected against the perceived value.

As the salesperson, you are in control of a big part of the real value, as you are in control of designing the experience. Ensure that you have great support, ensure you deliver on the promises you make, and you'll create rabid fans with every sale.

When Mindvalley were in the early years of online education products in personal growth, most companies didn't have strong after-sales support. Most of the industry was focused on online marketing (perceived value) and making huge profits in the process. When Mindvalley made the decision to create a "WOW team"—the customer-support arm that was responsible for WOWing the customer *after* the sale—we set a new standard in the industry. People would buy more and more because they knew the real value was there, and the support really made sure they got the results they were looking for.

You might have heard of the term "buyer's remorse." This is when a buyer judges the real value of the product to be less than the perceived value. Buyers will naturally tend to feel this regret post-purchase, making it all the more critical for the seller to measure the two different values accurately in order to dampen this effect for the buyer.

The Dark Side of Value-Based Selling

As the seller, you have the ability to manipulate the perceived value at your will. This is where you need to gut check your ethics gauge, because if you don't care about the client, you can lie and cheat the buyer into making the purchase. You need to be careful because doing this is not sustainable. It will take a toll on you, and it doesn't make anyone happier. You need to always ensure that you do not push the perceived value to exceed the real value. This is the sales sweet spot.

A FEW WORDS ABOUT COST

Everything has a cost. We already covered earlier elements of a transaction around time, energy, money, emotion, and risk. All of them put together will equal a certain cost you need to understand in the sales transaction. To illustrate this, I want to use an example that is close to my heart. I was selling meditation headphones. I purchased these from a reseller at sixty-five dollars apiece. This was my raw cost.

Yet to sell these headphones, there were more costs involved. I had to borrow money at interest rate to purchase a thousand of them. I also had to pay shipping costs. I then needed to keep them in a warehouse with monthly costs. I also wanted to sell them online, so I set up a Shopify store, which cost me monthly fees. I set up the business entity and the accounting system. I then had to write copy, build the website, and connect everything together. Finally, I had to market and sell it.

All of these elements brought that cost up. If you are in the business of trying to maximize your abundance and make the world a better place with your product, then you'll naturally want to look at cost as an area you want to minimize. The lower the cost, the higher your profit margin.

This seems like sound advice. However, you need to be very careful not to cut away the elements that drive the value up. In this example, I could have purchased headphones from another reseller that only cost ten dollars, yet the quality would've been at a much lower level. I could've chosen to sell them in person instead of online, or kept them in my own house instead of a warehouse. All these decisions needed to be measured in terms of how they expended or built energy.

As the business owner or salesperson, you do have some control over that cost. It's important here to note that sometimes when there is a sales problem, it's about increasing the costs instead of lowering them. In the case of my headphones, if I had bundled the headphones with a course that increased the cost, I might now have a completely new product with a new value, both real and perceived. This would've given me a massive opportunity to raise the price.

Always keep an eye on costs, and if you have pressures that are pushing you to lower them, it's great to always be renegotiating your process. Just be very mindful of the full impact of those decisions. One story I always hear is that when the economy dips, the first thing most companies do is cut their marketing budgets to save costs. However, if others are reducing their budgets, this means ad costs will be lower as a consequence. This results in a greater opportunity to take up market share if you happen to be in a cash-rich position. So when the recession hits, double down on your marketing and sales. When others retreat, it's time to charge.

WHAT IS THE RIGHT PRICE
FOR MY PRODUCT?

This is the easiest of all the variables to modify. As the salesperson, the price you sell the product is completely in your control. You can raise it or lower it. You can structure payment plans. There is so much room to move around with price, and it's entirely up to you to structure it in a way that lowers resistance, supports the perceived value, and allows the sale to happen.

Your job, when it comes to pricing, is to understand the client the best you can. You want to price your product at the highest point possible with consideration to real value. This way, you will ensure the client is going to be happy with the decision to buy. If your price is much higher than the real value, you might sell, but you will get unhappy customers. You won't stay in business too long.

If price is higher than perceived value, the sale will *not* happen in the first place. The good news is that perceived value can be modified quite easily with marketing and sales. Just ensure that you have a balance that creates fans.

The perfect sales market is:

Real value > perceived value > price > cost

Notice that with every single one of those variables, you are in control as the seller.

You can set the price. You can change the cost structures by modifying your product and supporting material. You can change the market positioning and sales strategy to increase the perceived value. You can even adjust the real value by understanding the needs of the buyer and modifying the product to match those needs.

In sum, you can deliver an amazingly valuable product to a buyer if:

1. You maximize the real value

2. You market so that the perceived value is higher than the price, yet lower than the real value

3. You minimize costs enough to stay profitable

When you look at it, it seems too simple. And, indeed, there are two variables that you do not control: the buyer and the market.

Dealing with External Forces

Each of the elements above are under the pressure of external forces. If your competitors can come along and, at a price lower than yours, make the same offer, then you might notice that buyers have now shifted their choice away from you.

You also face the fact that demands and expectations from buyers are getting higher and higher. This means that costs must go up to support the real-value expectations. At the same time, your price might be squeezed by the competition.

This is how a company like Amazon could succeed using levels of efficiency that are unmatched in the marketplace. Yet, they didn't begin fully dominant and wildly profitable. Their strategy was a bold one. They first looked to create the world's largest bookstore at the dawn of the internet. To achieve a successful business model with profit, it required taking a huge share of the market. In the beginning, investors were skeptical because year after year, Amazon was running a loss. Nonetheless, they came in and disrupted the purchase experience with the popularization of online shopping. This allowed for a more beautiful, fun, high-converting, and low-cost purchase experience. It was also more scalable than anything seen before. As the cost of technology dropped, the trust of buying online rose, and Amazon reached the height it has today, becoming the dominant player in the industry.

If you plan to sell something equal to what can be bought on Amazon, it will be a very difficult battle against a giant. Many will complain when it affects their businesses. Yet, the market serves what the buyers want. Better prices, better experience, better products.

Walmart did the same as it started creating superstores where you could buy anything you wanted. Smaller stores complained but failed to reinvent themselves to offer something superior to the buyers.

When shopping malls started decades before, a similar experience was felt by the smaller street-side stores who found themselves victims of these changes.

You'll want to be very aware of what it is that you are selling and what direction the market is going. The market is the only thing you don't have control over. Playing victim won't be a strategy for the long term. You'll need to keep your mind open to what problems you need to solve for the buyers and how you can deliver an experience that is different and more valuable.

When I started this business selling headphones for meditation, branded by Mindvalley, I went out and got a supplier from California that had such a premium product, made so ethically, I thought it would fly off the shelves. Wrong. The market was looking for a product that was much cheaper, and because of high competition, the perceived value was squeezed and strictly commoditized.

Now my cost was higher than my value, and I would need to sell at a loss for the product to move. Lesson learned.

This chapter is extremely important for you to understand how much power you hold as the seller. Every variable is under your control as you respond to markets and buyers. As you keep an eye on the market, you can see what can be done to ensure your product/service isn't in a category where it is about to be commoditized.

Here is a tip: if the product can be found on Amazon, you better have amazing branding, or else you will be undercut and outperformed very quickly.

As you get to know your clients better, you'll have a better understanding of which product/service features really drive up the perceived value. When I was eighteen years old and working at a family business selling swimming pools, the winter ended with lots of damage to many pools in the area. Sales came in fast as most people wanted to get their pools replaced. The best part was, the insurance companies were covering the costs. The employees and I all went to my father and shared the fact that competitors were selling pools at a lower price. They were selling many more pools than we were in the biggest rush of the decade. His decision was simple: "Let's raise the price even more."

Everyone (including me) thought he was crazy. Was he really looking to milk customers for as much money as possible in the middle of a crisis? I learned my lesson at a very young age, because when the dust settled and the rush was starting to die down, all our competitors had their calendars booked for the season, leaving any new customers to have to wait at least three months for a pool. Clients who came to us? Installation next week.

For the rest of the season, we had clients walk in looking for a pool to jump in *now*, when it was hot outside. We were able to serve this clientele with even more customer support, more attention to detail, and higher profit margins, allowing the business to grow and make more impact.

If the prices weren't so high, these niche customers (who also happened to be the best clients to have because they didn't mind paying a premium to get a great quality product) wouldn't have been able to get the pool their family was really looking forward to have that summer.

The price isn't about *your* ideas of value; it's about the buyer's. Remember that.

ACTION STEPS

1. Take a moment to look at products you already sell and think about why you charge the price you charge. If you notice that it's based on your cost, make a note of it and write out why you think you chose that method of pricing.

2. Think about the recent products you bought and what would have been the most you would have paid for it. When you bought it, were you conscious of your own perceived value of the product? After you bought it, did the real value make you love or hate the decision to buy it?

PART 2

LET'S START TALKING · ABOUT LOVE

WE SPENT THE FIRST PART OF THE BOOK REALLY GIVING YOU THE framework to understand sales. That was the foundation required to get to this part, where we are really going to put in the work required to get to the ultimate level of sales. It's all about selling with love.

There are five major "loves" that need to be reviewed in order to sell from love more consistently. I say more consistently because you will have moments where you might slip to lower emotions. This is not a conscious decision, but it will happen. Life events will change you. Certain clients will appear that will challenge your way of thinking.

This is all fine. The following chapters will serve as a blueprint to make you understand what it's like to sell each "love." They're going to give you practical processes you can follow to ensure that you stay more consistent in selling with love. If you ever slip to lower emotions, you'll have a checklist to come back to. This checklist will guide you to make the right corrections as issues arise.

This is no joke. Going through these five "loves" in selling will unlock an abundance like you've never seen before. With each step, you'll be getting out of your own way and truly seeing the magic in what you do (or the lack of it, with steps on how to fix it).

Let's get started.

CHAPTER 5

LOVE YOUR IMPACT

WITH EVERY SALE COMES A TRANSFORMATION. SOMETHING CHANGES. When the buyer agrees to buy and the transaction is complete, a shift occurs. Money usually leaves one account, and commitments are made. Someone's life changes. A problem is expected to be solved. Sometimes it's a big thing, and sometimes it isn't. The formula is never null. An impact will always be made as a result of making the sale.

When you sell, do you know what impact you have? Are you conscious of what motivates you to sell? I explained earlier that every sale is an energy exchange. If you are going to put any kind of energy into making a sale happen, it's good to have a level of awareness of what impact and purpose the sale will have.

LET'S START WITH SIMPLE LEMONADE

If you have no clue, it's time to step back and assess what's really happening. Let's take a simple example: a kid running a lemonade stand in the neighborhood. The kid who sells lemonade on the block is usually the proverbial example of young hustle. If you take a moment to look at the impact, you can see something basic happening: a client gets a drink that refreshes them.

This is already a great way to look at impact. But when you are in the position of being the seller and/or business owner, you can sometimes lose sight of that impact and be more focused on your own immediate needs. Perhaps the kid thinks, *I get money to buy stuff I want.*

All sellers love that impact! Heck, if you operate this lemonade shop for the summer, the kid will have more money than he would know how to spend (although there are always more ways to spend, right?).

Is there one that is better than the other here? It seems like the second reason is more selfish. But does that make the first one better?

No. This is something I've personally struggled with when I got into sales. I start thinking that the impact for others is more important than the impact for myself. But they are equally important. They are simply positioned from different perspectives. And if you don't have love for the impact from each point of view, you'll see that the balance will be off.

When You Care More about the Impact for Yourself than the Buyer

Let's say the kid only cares about money for themselves. He starts taking advantage of people. He charges a price higher than the real value, making the lemonade cheaper. He squeezes the most from each customer for the one and only goal: to increase profits.

Eventually, customers will be mad, and no more sales will happen. The kid might get a short-term gain, but it will pale in comparison to the potential their business could have had. Missing out on potential is the biggest loss that most people don't even see.

When You Care More about the Impact for the Buyer than Yourself

Now, let's say the opposite happens. The kid only cares about giving a refreshing drink to the client. Perhaps they would charge as little as possible for their lemonade to ensure the most amount of satisfaction per sale.

Again, we face a problem here. The kid might run out of money and eventually no longer be able to serve lemonade to anyone. Additionally, they couldn't expand their operations to a level where they could serve far more people.

This is why you need to keep in mind every level of impact. Lacking awareness and clarity on the ultimate impact of your sale limits the potential of what you can ultimately do to make the world a better place while reaching abundance at the same time.

Now, selling lemonade might be just a fun little project for the summer, but how would you feel if you were driving by and the kid gave you this speech:

"Hey! Thanks for stopping by and supporting my project to inspire and educate the whole neighborhood. See, many kids are left alone during the summer while their parents are gone to work. So I started this lemonade business to serve refreshing drinks to everyone. Many kids in the area get to come and learn about sales and running a small business. It keeps everyone busy, we have lots of fun, and we get to grow and learn in the process. We appreciate your support, and you'll find the drink absolutely amazing. How many would you like to buy?"

In that statement lies a clue to the way of selling with love. A hint: it goes beyond the buyer and the seller.

What Happened in Beverly Park, on *Shark Tank*, and with Wheelchairs

While looking into this simple idea, I was amazed to find three examples of selling with love at work.

In 2012, at Beverly Park Elementary School in Michigan, they decided to create buzz with the concept of lemonade stands. In an effort to teach entrepreneurship and sales, they set out to achieve a Guinness World Record for the longest chain of lemonade stands. In the process, they inspired the whole community to come together and support the goal. People were more drawn to contribute to this initiative than if they had just set up a corner stand. Impact was maximized in the process, and they did, in fact, set a new world record.[6]

In my second example, Jack Bonneau was only eleven years old when he pitched the idea of franchising lemonade stands on *Shark Tank* in 2016.[7] Here was someone who took the basic concept and thought, *What if I provide the right system for young entrepreneurs to maximize their sales with lemonade? A much bolder vision impacting many more lives?* I looked into what Jack is doing now. He continues to create businesses to enable youth and teens to do inspiring things. He even has a TEDx Talk worth watching![8]

Finally, eleven-year-old Zack Francom decided to open up a lemonade stand in his hometown of Provo, Utah to buy wheelchairs for people. With an impact goal at the center of his business, the stand was able to generate considerable sales and PR support from

---

6 "Longest Line of Lemonade Stands," *Guinness Book of World Records*, https://www.guinnessworldrecords.com/world-records/103193-longest-line-of-lemonade-stands.

7 Robyn D. Shulman, "How 12-Year-Old Jack Bonneau from *Shark Tank* Is Leading the Way for Kid Entrepreneurs," *Forbes*, February 23, 2018, https://www.forbes.com/sites/robynshulman/2018/02/23/how-12-year-old-jack-bonneau-from-shark-tank-is-leading-the-way-for-kid-entrepreneurs/?sh=175d9487521c.

8 Jack Bonneau, "Kids Can Be Role Models," TEDx Boulder, June 2018, https://www.ted.com/talks/jack_bonneau_kids_can_be_role_models.

local news channels. He was able to have over three hundred wheel-chairs donated from the money raised from his lemonade stand![9]

People want to buy when they clearly understand why you're selling. And the bigger the why, the bigger the pie.

THE WHY IS KEY:
IDENTIFYING THREE IMPACTS

Why do you get up and do what you do every day? Is there a point to all of it? I'd like to assume that if you picked up this book, you know there is more to life than just being here to take what you can and leaving the world in whatever condition when you're done.

I believe we are all here for the ultimate experience of making some positive impact. The more conscious you are about what that im-pact is, the more you can feel aligned to your purpose in life. Now, depending on how old or young you are, this could seem like a big deal.

But don't worry. The goal isn't to have ultimate clarity and certainty. The process itself is a continuous journey of discovery. Action is the tool that moves you forward.

---

9   Cathy Free, "Zack Francom Sells Lemonade to Buy Wheelchairs for Those Who Need Them," *People*, June 26, 2014, https://people.com/human-interest/zack-francom-sells-lem-onade-to-buy-wheelchairs-for-those-who-need-them/.

1. Buyer Impact

What problem are you solving for the buyer? This is the main reason for going into a sales process. Your first duty is to make the life of your potential buyer better through doing business with you. It's going to be quite impossible to use any of the concepts from this book if your product doesn't solve any problems. This can be a common oversight for people with the best of intentions when they get a little too excited about the product they created.

I was completing a workshop led by Tucker Max, an amazing businessman and writer. He's written multiple *New York Times* bestsellers and now looks to invest in business startups. In the workshop, he repeated the mantra I've been sharing so far that is so important: "When I see people asking for money who are only in love with their product, I don't invest. I want them to be in love with solving a problem. Those are the people who make successful businesses."

The product can be loved, yes, but it isn't the first love. Impact—solving problems—is where your first loyalty lies when selling with love.

How clear are you on the impact you make in the life of your buyer?

List of examples:

- In real estate, you create simplicity, trust, and savings in time and/or money for people who are looking to buy or sell a property.

- As an agency, you offer reliable, cost-effective, scalable products and services to other businesses.

- As a retail/e-commerce business, you provide available access to goods in a timely fashion.

We launched a new kind of event at Mindvalley called Mindvalley U. It was a one-month-long event with amazing speakers, thousands of attendees, and lots of fun, too. One of the keynote speakers I had invited to join was Verne Harnish. He is an incredible entrepreneur and author who really drives home ideas on making people successful in building and scaling businesses. When he took the stage, he reminded everyone about the simplest, most universal mission statement for every single business:

"We aim to make X easier."

Make sure this impact is crystal clear. How does dealing with you make whatever challenge that lies ahead easier for the buyer?

- Amazon makes it easier to buy online.

- Tesla is making it easier to own an electric car.

- Microsoft makes it easier for every household to have a PC.

What is your easy statement?

As explained by Verne Harnish, the easy statement is a phrase that explains the purpose of your business based on how you make a certain process easier for your clients.

Example: an easy statement of "Impact and Integrity" means that you make it easier for companies to grow in revenue by working with a team of consultants that have ready solutions for the most common roadblocks in growing businesses.

Always start with the problems you solve for the clients. What's the buyer impact you want to make?

2. Seller Impact

When you are building a company that requires you to sell (raise money, hire talent, market and sell the products/services), or if you are in a sales position within an established company, you should list all the ways you want to make an impact for *yourself*:

- Are you looking to make more money?

- Are you looking to learn more skills?

- Do you seek recognition for the work you do?

- Do you want to feel better about yourself?

- Do you have something to prove to yourself or others?

You don't need to rank these ideas or label them as good or bad, egocentric or unselfish. Simply take inventory of every impact you are looking to make for yourself from the moment you get up in the morning, doing what you do.

3. World Impact

When you start with impact, you can really look into what legacy you want to leave. You will have a compass that can guide you on all the major decisions that will follow. Keep in mind that this is highly personal. What works for you might not for someone else, and that's perfectly fine.

Let me tell you a story. Years after graduation, one of my former classmates found employment with an up-and-coming e-cigarette company. He was one of their first employees, and they were looking for a VP of Sales at the time. He reconnected with me to see if I was interested in taking on the position. It would have come with a massive salary and stock options. Plus, it seemed like an exciting product to sell: new in the marketplace, better than any competitor, and consumers *loved* it.

Well, *of course* they did. The product delivered large amounts of nicotine and was highly addictive.

This is why being clear on impact is so important. When faced with a decision like this, you need to be very clear on why you would say yes. I didn't show any interest in the position, as I knew that my success in this role could lead to far more people being addicted to a substance I didn't think the world needed more of.

I wanted my core contribution to involve making the world a place where good people get to sell good products. This would minimize and/or eliminate bad salespeople selling scammy products that take advantage of people. I was clear on that. This made my decision very easy.

However, the choice was highly personal. For someone else, the same motive to help others could easily lead them to different actions. Consider that vaping is less harmful than smoking and can sometimes help people quit. What if a buyer had been a smoker for twenty years, and the only way they could get off cigarettes was by switching over to this e-cigarette?

Looking into my own family, my mother had been a smoker since the age of twelve. Of course, back then, the negative health effects of cigarettes was highly downplayed. I had a few of these vaporizers and brought them over for her to try. Using these, she was able to massively reduce the number of cigarettes she smoked in a day. She felt her sense of taste come back and felt better in the process. Sure, it's not as perfect as quitting, yet it was a powerful start, and I'm so proud of her.

Let's say, as a seller, I wanted to get more people to make the switch to less harmful vaping instead of smoking. I knew that I could help push for that cause within the company. In that case, saying yes to that position would be reasonable as well.

The crucial question is, how clear are you on the world impact that matters to you?

Start big picture. Yes, this part might not seem directly connected to your sales problem. Yet, it's crucial because if alignment isn't happening here, it can lead you astray in both your personal and professional life.

It's time to put aside all concerns about your specific work and think about what is truly important to you, especially when it comes to a global contribution. Forget about how individually capable you are right now and simply go to the essence of what drives you.

- What is a problem you wish could be solved in the world?

- What is something currently happening in the world that you find is unacceptable?

- What is a change you think the world needs?

- If you were granted one wish and it had to make the world a better place, what would it be?

You might be trying to find that perfect statement in response to these questions. That's not the point. I want you to start making a list first. It can be very long, too. Don't make any judgments of the goals you set. This is *your* list.

Once you have that put together, try to rank them.

Starting with the top one, take a moment to write a paragraph answering the following question: why is that problem important to you?

Do this for the top three in your list.

What usually happens is that you'll notice a personal story emerges for why that topic is important to you. In my case, I know there is a part of me that wants to rid the world of manipulative marketers and salespeople who take advantage of others. I personally appreciate how destructive their behavior can be because I know how it feels to be on the receiving end of it. Looking back at how I was involved myself, I don't want anyone else to go through what I did.

You don't have to solve all the world's problems—just the one that's most important to you. Looking at the list of sustainability goals from the UN, for instance, I find them all very powerful. To name a few: no poverty; zero hunger; climate action; and industry, innovation, and infrastructure.[10]

I want to see many, if not all of them, solved. Yet, when I think about a global problem that is more personal to me, I light up differently. It feels like my soul's calling.

This practice is not to be taken lightly. Once you get clear on that, you will be able to see how the rest of the work you do ties everything together. But it has to start with the problem.

---

10   "The 17 Goals," United Nations, https://sdgs.un.org/goals.

By doing this exercise, you become clearer on what you want to see solved. If you keep this as your North Star for all the decisions you make, you will always be selling from a place of love.

World Impact in Scarcity

I've had times where I was trying to make ends meet. The bank account was looking thin, I had to cut on expenses, and I could barely give myself the space to start thinking about others while I was trying to put myself back together.

Understandably, it was hard to embrace this idea of world impact when my own basic needs weren't being met. I remember sharing my ideas on making a world impact with a friend of mine who works as a humanitarian and runs an NGO. He gave me the perspective of those working in the streets of a poor country. They weren't able to care about the world or the client because they were focused on feeding their family and surviving.

Fair point. Also, it put into perspective that my "troubles" were not as grand as I made myself think they were. Abundance is the solution to scarcity. I know I can't suggest to others what their priorities should be, but I've always noticed that when I find myself giving more care and attention to the impact on others over the impact on myself, it always pays back. I can go out there and sell from love, focused so strongly on the problems I want to solve for others. It quickly makes me realize that I can be happy with so little. I feel like I can truly make a difference. And the abundance seems to come back naturally.

Not bad.

Imagine what the world would look like if everyone with influence, power, and impact started to sell from love and cared about their full impact. Let's bring Amazon back as an example.

Sure, they are doing wonders for buyers. They are creating an efficient marketplace. Yet, what are they doing for their employees? Do they consider the impacts for them? What about the small businesses that get taken out because Amazon undercut them? Can they show care for them, too?

I can't go too far into the details of what Amazon does. But I know that they started creating marketplaces for third-party sellers to join the e-commerce boom. I know they make efforts to reduce packaging so there is less waste. I don't think it's by chance that they find themselves as one of most valuable companies in the world. They are not perfect, that is for sure. Yet, it looks to me like there is more care than ever before.

We live in some of the most abundant times, when there are more opportunities than ever. Now more people can realize that when you choose a bigger mission with a bigger impact, you start making decisions that lift you into abundance. I know for me, it's always a little scary to set a bold mission to impact more lives. Yet from that decision, bigger actions get taken and more lives can be improved, including my own.

If you are currently reading this book, this means you are looking for a way to make a bigger impact. You want to align your sales activities to your purpose. And when you get clear on the impact, you'll have the fuel it takes to work through the hard times and get the results you want.

You do not need to compromise your ethics to sell more. Instead, you can use your ethics to enhance conversions. That's the point!

When I consult companies on sales, it's amazing how easy the sales become when I explain to them why I'm selling. One of my clients, the CEO of a beauty company in Malaysia, told me about all the problems in her industry. People lie. People shame their clients into purchasing more. They use high-pressure tactics and make everyone feel bad in the process. She wanted to do things differently. I explained to her my exact vision of how I want to see sales happen in the world. She had a glow in her eyes and related to this vision so strongly that she asked how she could hire me as a consultant. She wanted to be a part of that future. That's the kind of interaction you want to have.

Now, once you get clear on the world impact, you want to start breaking down all the other impacts that come from the result of you selling a product or service. Eventually, you'll see the impact on the buyer and on yourself, and the next chapters will cover that. What I want you to do now is list all the other people who will be affected by your decision to sell what you are about to sell.

As you make the list, consider which categories each person belongs in:

- The world

- My community

- My family

- My colleagues

- People who follow me, etc.

This is the gravy that will make all your marketing and sales material shine. Yet, it goes even beyond that—it's really where the heart of what you do exists.

That's why, in the next chapter, we explore why loving the client is so important.

This Book Can Have a Global Impact

As a result of me selling my book on *impact* and *integrity*, I will see my impact on...

The world.

Helping good businesses learn how to sell with love allows them to grow, thrive, and become examples of what happens when you sell from such a powerful place. It also gives buyers better choices to buy from companies they truly believe in. This makes the marketplace more efficient and more transparent and allows abundance to overflow to more members of society.

I believe salespeople inside organizations can be catalysts to positive change by showing stakeholders the potential of expanding responsibility, making better products that are more aligned with the values of the company and bringing authenticity and transparency to the sales process.

As a bonus effect, people who become informed of these ideas start being more conscious as buyers. This, in effect, shifts their purchase behavior to support the organizations they believe in, which helps selling with love to thrive even more. This process is a great accelerator of positive change across all industries.

ACTION STEPS

1. What is your easy statement?

2. Take a moment to gain your clarity on impact. As a result of me selling X, what does the buyer, the seller (or myself), or the world at large get?

3. Use the clarity from the answers above to see how your marketing material reflects these truths.

CHAPTER 6

LOVE YOUR CLIENT

After working at Mindvalley for about two years, I was working in a new division. In the past, I was part of the entrepreneurship division, selling products on marketing, sales, business building, and more.

Now I was asked to work on a whole new product line. I didn't feel so confident because I could barely define what the product was. It was called energy healing sessions. I started reading more about what this was exactly: a webinar with a psychic healer who would guide a meditation, setting a theme and clearing the energy for those who joined.

Upon reading about it, I was skeptical, but I was willing to experience it for myself. I logged into a call, and I was left...unchanged.

I got a little scared. I didn't really believe in the effects of this program. I wouldn't want to sell something that didn't have a positive impact.

This can be a common mistake we make as salespeople. We try to judge the value of a product/service based on the value we perceive. I caught myself, in this case, assuming I was the client. To correct this mistake, I applied one of the basic activities in marketing and sales: market research.

I found the contact details of the people who had bought this program in the past. I reached out and told them I wanted to talk. I wanted to understand who they were and why this program was important to them.

After just a few conversations, I was blown away.

One former customer was Lucy. I asked her a series of questions that would provide data for my market research. She owned a flower shop in Tampa, Florida. She was in her late forties. Divorced with one daughter.

"Lucy, I'd love to know more about why you decided to sign up for the energy clearing sessions. What were you looking for?" I asked.

She said, "I felt like I was stuck. I wanted to see more results in my business. Things feel up and down sometimes in my life. I feel sad about how distant I am from my nineteen-year-old daughter, for example. She lives in a different city, and at the time, we were not very close. It seemed like there was a gap between us, and I wanted to do something for us to get closer. This program felt like a great system to try."

"This information is great, Lucy. Now, this was one year ago, right? What happened once you completed the twelve sessions?"

I could feel her smiling as she talked now.

"It's been so amazing. I get to join every month. The process is fun, meditative, and stress relieving. I always feel great once it's done. I've become a more patient and accepting person. Best part is, I've had my daughter join a session with me as well. She enjoyed it, too! We have been getting closer over this past year, and I'm really glad I decided to do these sessions."

It was beautiful. How priceless is that? I was quickly reminded I wasn't simply selling energy clearing sessions to Lucy—I was giving her the tool to repair the relationship with her daughter. That was worth lots of money. Her real value from these sessions was massive. Her perceived value was very high as well. The price was just under that, which gave the business a good profit margin.

Now I knew that with the extra profits, I could afford to pay for ads that targeted more Lucys in the world to get this kind of healing.

I felt inspired, and these stories continued to surface. One that really stood out was Chuck, a man in his late thirties. Chuck was a very special case, and bless him for being so vulnerable with me. He was seeing a therapist and having trouble keeping a regular job. He was facing some bouts of depression and anxiety in the workplace. When he discovered these healing sessions, he felt something so profound that it shifted his very core.

"Jason, it's crazy," he said to me over the phone. "These sessions come through to me like a happiness booster pill. My therapist agrees that it's been highly beneficial for me. I've reduced my medication, and I'm happy to report that I've been holding my new employment and I love it. I'm so glad I learned about this healing program. It changed my life."

Hearing this story shifted my attitude. Can you imagine if I had stuck to my original story? Just because this product didn't do anything for me? If I had merely continued selling and marketing this product during a launch, without doing research, I wouldn't have found these persuasive testimonies. Instead, I would have felt a little embarrassed. Those shame-guilt blockages would have popped up. And fewer people like Lucy and Chuck would've had a chance to discover this program that would transform their lives, simply because of my own immediate biases and limitations.

Forget for a second what financial impact you have on the company. Forget for a second how your performance would be questioned if you hesitated to sell. Let's focus, instead, on the client.

YOU ARE NOT THE CLIENT

When you determine the value of a product based only on your own perceptions, you are making a quick, lazy decision. If you don't take the time to know whom you are selling to and the impact you have on them, then you will start making some terrible assumptions. And if you do continue to sell in this way, then you allow your limited ideas on the value to outweigh those of your client. I always make sure to check in with myself to put my own assumptions aside before selling.

I'm thinking of the kid who loves his fish so much that he takes it out of the water and gives it a big hug…and it dies. The child was too hasty and did not take the time to understand the basic needs of the fish.

The best way to love is to understand. When you start to sell your product and service, you want to start to get to know your client. The same goes if you want to help people who remind you of the younger version of yourself, such as in the business of teaching: don't ignore any of the data sent by actual customers, even if it's tempting to assume they are just like you. I'm all for trusting your intuition, but our egos can sometimes make us blind to the realities of our business. When arrogance is at play, even unwittingly, it can prevent us from helping real people.

LOVE IS UNDERSTANDING: CREATING YOUR BUYER AVATAR

This is where you'll often hear about needing a "client avatar." There are other names used in the industry: personas, target buyer, and so forth. What you need to know is how you can create a demographic and psychographic analysis for the person you want to sell to. What are their problems, their aspirations? What does their day-to-day life look like? This should help you identify better language to use with them, be more relevant, and as a result, help you sell more, too.

If you are like me, it's something you dread to do. It takes energy. You might think you already know. But trust me, you will open the floodgates of abundance and massive action if you start with this step. For instance, I remember sitting on the fence about writing this very book. Then I got clear on my client. I got clear on exactly why it was important for me to do this. I knew the impact I wanted to make from step 1, the first "love." Through this process, I got to know my client very intimately.

There are a few key ways to approach this.

First, you can send surveys to your past customers. You ask demographic questions like age, occupation, location, and everything else that will let you identify more of who they are. This works especially if you have a large volume of customers; you can start to spot trends and get closer to who seems to be the clients you serve.

But this isn't my preferred approach. The second one, I think, truly unlocks the magic. Plus, it is more accessible if you don't have existing clients...yet.

Take a moment to think about the most perfect, ideal client you have served in the past.

If you are already in business, there must be an existing client you serve that makes you light up. When this person buys from you, you get excited, and you deliver the ultimate service or product with joy. You know you've transformed their lives by making the sale.

How much time have you spent to really get to know them? This is an important exercise to do. You want to know everything about them. Get on a call and ask them the questions that allow you to build something much more important than demographics. You want to understand what is important to them. Why do they make certain decisions? What is the mission/vision of their company or their life? What do they stand for? What do they stand against?

When you are selling a product or service, you are trying to communicate to your potential clients why it will serve them to buy. Before you sell to them, understand their story. Make them feel seen and heard, and actually take notes. A lack of understanding will greatly affect sales.

If you don't have this ideal customer in mind or you are just getting started, I want you to do the same exercise, only this time, you can imagine an imaginary buyer. That perfect client walking over to you. As funny as this might sound to you, it's actually going to help you get clear on whom you really want to serve, without restrictions.

Imagine having to write a letter to your target audience. In my case here, it was an email to all the people I found who might be interested in energy clearing sessions. Thankfully, my client Chuck could help me there. Publishing actual stories by clients like him helps people get engaged in sales copy. You'll learn more about this in Chapter 8. Once I had gathered a full story from Chuck's transformation, I included it in the email I sent to my list. (To see my email with Chuck, go to jasonmarccampbell.com/chuck and you'll be able to read it yourself.)

After we sent out this email, I went into the system that gave me all the fancy information on what recipients did with it. Open rates were up. I could see people spent more time reading it. Finally, people clicked the link and bought the seven-dollar trial at a high rate.

When you take time to love the client, you first take time to understand them. Once you fully understand them, you can see if the impact you are looking to create in the world will serve them.

When you know it will, this is when you can start to make sure your specific product best serves them.

HELPING EVERYONE IS HELPING NO ONE

If there's one thing I realize in this world, it's that we're all a little crazy and trying to make sense of this whole experience as humans. Having been in the personal growth industry for so long, I've met many coaches and teachers who want to help people with their mindset. When it comes to selling, here's a common mindset people have for loving your client:

I want to help everyone with my product/service. I don't want to exclude anyone.

In a way, this is true. Yet, the problem with having no focus on your client niche is that with no precision, no one will relate to you. If I'm a client, I want to feel like the solution I buy is tailored to the unique "me"!

If you, the seller, advertise by saying, "It works for everyone," then I don't feel like you understand me, the buyer. As a matter of fact, I might even judge your claim. Everyone is different, and if someone claims to help everyone, then the impact is lost.

You need a bull's-eye. If you play darts without a board or a bull's-eye, you'll only hit the wall, right? Instead, you have a target. Your target, in this case, is the ultimate, perfect lead who walks into your life, looking for your product or service. Feel free to exaggerate how perfect this person is. Once formed in your mind, look for the solution to their potential problems.

This is what having an avatar is. After you make one, unless you are an amazing darts player, you'll probably be hitting around the bull's-eye more often than on it—and that's great. That's exactly the idea. You score points, and people will still identify with what you're speaking about, even if they are not exactly the avatar you targeted.

This can be particularly liberating, especially when you're just getting started and don't have enough past customers to provide the marketing data required. Start with the ideal, and you can gather more data as you move forward.

DEALING WITH NEGATIVE CLIENTS

You might have a case in which you have an angry or demanding client. That one client who never seems to be happy. You might be thinking, *Oh my God, I wish that client would just leave me alone!*

That would be a terrible mistake. If you want to reach the ultimate levels of love in selling, this is an opportunity for one of the biggest breakthroughs you could have. If you get this type of client, you need to realize that this person has the potential to become your biggest raving fan.

How? When they complain this much, it's usually because they believe so strongly in your product that they want it to be even better. Unfortunately, in a given moment, you might not have the mental bandwidth to discuss product innovation, so you might interpret your client's comment as merely a complaint. Do not make the mistake of taking that complaint at face value. Instead, what is more likely at play here is that the client doesn't feel understood. Underneath the griping, they are trying to get attention and feel relevant. They believe in your product and impact, yet they feel like you don't care.

Most client complaints will be spurred from the feeling that you, the seller, don't care.

> **Sidenote:** This tip is also very effective in relationships. The only arguments I've had with my romantic partner involved perceptions of the other person not showing care. Or making assumptions about intent. And overall, forget-

ting to *listen*. Perhaps the next book should be about how to use sales to find love. ☺

Caring takes time. Caring takes energy. Yet, so does complaining and being angry. The worst clients are the ones who don't buy and don't care. If the client takes the time to complain, it's because they are willing to use energy to express their concern. Let's go back to the formula:

Real value > perceived value > price > cost

If they complain before they buy, then you need to spend time with that client to understand their needs and wants. What problem are they looking to solve? How relevant is that problem? How big and painful is that problem? What will their life look like once the problem is solved? Getting all this information will allow you to design your marketing and sales material to better serve—and better love— your customer. In the process, this increases the product's perceived value.

If the client complains after they buy, you need to mind the gap between perceived value and real value. You did a great job making them realize that buying this product was worth it for the price. But the product doesn't live up to the promises you made. This could be a product issue, which we will discuss later. Or it could also be a case of not getting clear on what this particular buyer valued.

Say you have thousands of people sign up for a Spartan Race. I remember when I did it the first time. I was completely new to the sport of obstacle course racing. It looked like fun, it looked like a challenge, and I was ready to try. So I did the race. It was painful. I spent three days with my knees really messed up. I had to go to the clinic for the entire week because I ripped the skin off my hands so badly from sliding down a rope climb. I had to change the bandages daily.

During the race, I thought it would never end! I was exhausted. My knees were killing me as I had not prepared to run in the process. I am grateful that I ran into my good friend Neil on the track. I remember trying to keep up with him and being frustrated that I couldn't keep up. Under the hot sun, I realized that I didn't apply enough sunscreen. I just wanted to go hide in the bushes in my mind and wait for nightfall. Yet, I persevered. I finished the race covered in mud, with sunburn on my arms and cuts everywhere, too.

And yet for some crazy reason, I kept signing up for more. I absolutely love the adventure, the challenge, the recognition of the tribe, jumping over fire. I am the ideal client. And there are enough people like me to have made Spartan racing a worldwide phenomenon.

I try to explain to my family why I do it, but they don't understand. They would never buy such an experience. To them, it sounds like torture and pain for no purpose. But there are some interesting differences between me and them. I'm highly competitive, and I'm always doing physically intense sports. They don't. My sister Tracy does outdoor activities, yet purposefully rolling in the mud is not her idea of a good time. Both my parents are not in physical shape to do such a challenge, and my little sister Jamie much prefers a good workout in air-conditioning.

This is fine. They are not the ideal clients for Spartan Races at this time.

This is an example of feedback from a nontarget avatar. Perceived value < price. In this case, Spartan should not listen to this feedback. It would be like asking a vegan to comment on the quality of meat in the restaurant.

I had a friend Ezekiel who did it, and he never wants to do it again. At first, he was really excited about the training. He was excited about buying the ticket. When he finished the race, he thought, *Wow, that was crazy, and I never want to do this again.* He is more about martial arts. He can never stop talking about the joys of Brazilian Jiu-Jitsu and "rolling" with other guys. In this case, we both have a similar profile, yet a different preference. That's very normal.

This was an example of an avatar that was far from the bull's-eye. He was actually happy to have done it but will not be a repeat buyer. His feedback could be included, but I would note that this particular friend decided to do his first race in the Beast category after my highly persuasive invitation. I'm sorry, Ezekiel (but not sorry as well).

Finally, you have me, the perfect avatar for Spartan Race.

This is why getting clear on your niche is extremely important. Once you've got this down, you don't need to change a product when just a few people aren't particularly happy with it. You'll get some people who trickle into your program and they might not be the perfect fit. But you will always have your core base.

The real value will change based on the client. If you know the ideal client you want to serve, then you can always test if someone isn't buying or if someone isn't happy after buying. Then you can make sure if it's a process, product, or client issue.

Should you try to make everyone happy? No. You should try to speak to the very target people you want to help. As your business grows, your target will get wider. You'll be able to spare the resources to optimize the real value and perceived value for the wider niches. But don't lose track of the target.

CREATING ADDITIONAL "CLIENT AVATARS"

Looking back on the Spartan Race example, I was the kind of client typical of their main avatar. This is the kind of person looking for an intense experience. I competed in age group and elite classes. In these, if you failed an obstacle, you needed to do thirty burpees on camera. If you didn't do it perfectly, you got a time penalty.

Spartan wants to create Olympic-level athletes as a goal. However, they decided they also want to get millions of people to do the race. Now they've created something called an open class in which people who want to run for fun can do so.

It's great. You can help each other out, and no one monitors your burpee count. People take selfies on the obstacles. If all of this happened at the same time the elite runners competed, Spartan would lose their core audience. Instead, they let all the open-class people go last in the day so they don't get in the way of the other athletes.

The company is huge now and has a massive following of rabid fans. They serve multiple types of clients, and they make sure each type understands the differences. The result? All are served amazingly well.

Yet, don't jump steps here and get ahead of yourself. It's best to start with one kind of client first. If you start with more, you'll end up not having that focus needed in the beginning, and it takes more capital. After you've got that down, you can include more without losing that base.

Even at Mindvalley where I worked, we had too many avatars at one point. When we decided to focus everything on serving the one avatar, it allowed us to focus extremely well. We then got ready to bring on more identities *only after* the primary one was getting saturated.

Loving your client is not just an affirmation or a quote you can put up on a wall. It's a dedication to actions, including understanding and listening. When you make this a habit, you are now on your way to being a great salesperson who will be respected, loved, and appreciated for all you do.

That's really how to love the client. And one of the best ways to demonstrate that love is to extend it to the actual product and service you give to them. The sales process doesn't end with the money in your hands—it only just begins.

ACTION STEPS

1. Think of the absolute perfect lead who might come to you for purchase. Write the story of who they are, what problem they face, and how excited they are to buy the product/service you are offering.

2. If you have existing clients, book a time to get on a call with them and ask questions about why they bought and who they are. You'll start to gain insights about what to focus on.

3. Set a reminder six months from now to revisit this chapter and go back to having more conversations with clients, refining what you know and building more stories.

4. Bonus action step: if one of the stories of transformation really impacted you, document it in the form of a story and use it during a sales conversation, in your marketing, and more.

CHAPTER 7

LOVE YOUR PRODUCT

Picture this recent scene of my life.

I maybe heard a few rumors about what was going to happen. But of course, I hadn't talked to anyone about it. September has just started, and everything is okay in my life. Yet, there is an announcement made that I told myself I wouldn't care about.

I check Google News. Is it good? Is it bad? Ah! It's got my attention. In the coming weeks, I have a slight feeling of missing out. I'm not feeling as efficient, and there is a deep desire I have for getting something new. Something…glorious. Something…unique.

It's not the first time this has happened. In fact, it feels like it happens every year. I had resisted all the other years. But now as November rolls in, I decide to take the plunge. It feels amazing.

I get home while carrying a white bag with a little box inside. I sit down and look at this carefully crafted box. It's beautiful. It's like Christmas when I finally see it. It's mine.

I just bought an iPhone 11 Max Pro. The purchase experience on Apple's part was ridiculous. It was not something that happened by accident. The whole thing had been predicted, planned, and executed with precision by their salespeople. No wonder Apple is one of the most valuable companies in the world. They absolutely love their product, and they keep making it better. Now that I have one myself, I absolutely love it, too. The battery is long lasting. It's fast. The screen is big. It's all wonderful. I had no issues from the moment I bought it.

In three years, I'll probably be sad about the product and ready to buy the next one. The cycle continues. And Apple is getting better at it every time. This is a company that is so product obsessed that they always carry their knowledge of client love as they continue down the road with product love.

Now, one part of that experience I remember really well is the gentleman who helped me purchase the phone. I was in an Apple store in Miami, and he was the coolest guy ever! First off, there was no pressure at all. He answered my questions about the trade-in value of my current phone. I had concerns over the price for additional data. He made a case for why we should try to save money and get a phone with the least data capacity. (I had iCloud, so I didn't need much data.)

This man seemed to anticipate my emotions of wanting the phone, being excited about it, being worried about choosing poorly. The whole time, he was helpful and fun to deal with. This is one style of sales I think works wonderfully for Apple. I can't help but contrast it with the times I bought phones over the past ten years at mobile phone shops where the employees were so high pressure and focused on making a sale. It would be a dreadful experience. Apple understood this pain and created an experience that is rare to find elsewhere.

I bought the new iPhone from this salesman. We became buddies, actually, and I gave him a recommendation on where to get vegan tacos. I *loved* being sold to by him! Because he loved the product so much, he kept sharing more about his experience with the phone. His enthusiasm rubbed off on me, and I was hooked. I wanted that experience, too!

When you absolutely love the product you sell, there is a new kind of energy in the air. You start to speak about it during the sales process with a kind of joy that is transferred directly to the buyer. If you look at most fundamental sales training, it focuses on the enthusiasm you can radiate to make people more excited to buy. Loving the product can make you have that natural radiance. It's highly contagious and effective.

Think about when a friend starts a new relationship. They share all the wonderful things their partner does for them, how they are different, how they have a spark, how they could even be *the one*. Everyone loves and remembers that feeling. When you want to get a product moving, your ability to sell from that energy level will work magic. The beauty of it is, you don't need to be Apple to do it. This is something you can achieve yourself quite fast, and it will apply to any industry.

DON'T FIGHT AN UPHILL BATTLE
WITH A BAD PRODUCT

Loving your product is so important. The opposite is going to hold you back from any success in selling it. Can you imagine having to work a sales position in which you need to sell problems? When people come to you, you give them more struggles in their lives. Whom would you sell to? If they did buy, how would you feel about the fact that you played a part in creating more trouble in their lives?

You would hesitate. You would try not to engage. You would feel drained after the day is over. You would be thrown into some serious shame-guilt blockages. That's how many people struggle with selling a product they dislike but need to sell. They are not convinced that the real value will be as expected, so they fear the negative consequences of a sale gone bad.

I love the following example because some people do *seem* to sell problems as part of their job. Look at escape rooms around the world—a problem to solve is pretty much what gets sold. You throw people in a room that is locked up and they can't get out unless they find the clues and solve the puzzles. But what they're really selling is an experience—a challenge, a burst of adrenaline in an urgent but safe situation, a unique bonding time with friends.

What is most important here is making sure you don't feel like you are selling a broken product. There is nothing worse than having to sell something according to a rule book that sets the perceived value so much higher than the real value. To avoid this, there is a clear way you can run an audit on your product.

INTEGRITY IS THE KEY

I remember going to a seminar during which the speaker was preaching, "When you get started in business, you need to fake it until you make it." I have to admit, I've used this approach in my life for little things, like public speaking in college. Back then, when people had to form groups for a project, I would tell everyone that I was great at public speaking. People were all terrified of it. They wanted me on their teams so I could take care of that part.

Actually, I was terrified of it. But it was something I wanted to overcome, so I used this "fake it until you make it" approach. Eventually, with all the practice, I got good at it and the aspiration became a reality. Since the stakes were not too high, I never really felt bad about doing this.

Problems only arise when your actions start to hurt other people. At its core, "fake it until you make it" is a tactic that relies on deception for your own benefit. If there are any negative effects from the sale in which you faked it until you made it, the unanticipated, negative cost will be distributed to the buyers as recipients of the lie. This will take away your brand credit and reputation.

Does "fake it until you make it" work? In some capacity, yes. It's the equivalent of making a deal with the devil, trading a long-term loss for a short-term gain. You end up "selling your soul." I would rather recommend a much more powerful system.

Don't fake it. Make it. And fix the product.

Sounds like a simple prescription, right? Well, on the surface, it is. If you don't love the product when you sell it, you probably have some ideas of what the product's shortcomings are. What are they? What can you do to fix them? Think about all the energy you spend to sell a product you don't think is good enough. First off, it takes more energy per sale to make it work. Your number of sales is actually lower than it could be, so you convert less. Finally, when you do sell, you might not be creating raving fans per sale. You are actually breaking the second step of Chapter 6—love the client—if you sell them a product inferior to what they expect.

All of this is no good and a waste. If you instead spend some time fixing the product, then you will see how you can make the business grow in sales. Clients will be extremely happy because you delivered your absolute best, backing a product you know is better.

That brings us to the other side of the spectrum. How good is good enough? If you are like me, you might get a case of sales resistance because you don't think your product is perfect. You might be always working on product improvement and never feeling like it's ready to sell. If you fall into this category, hang on—you'll see in Chapter 9 that the final "love" is the root of your problem.

WHAT TO DO WITH NEW PRODUCTS

As I mentioned earlier, integrity is the first key. If you are just starting out, you might be comparing yourself to large corporations and thinking you can't deliver as well as them. What you would be forgetting is the agility and attention to detail you can give when you truly spend the time to love your client. You can provide more value in different ways. Even if your product isn't perfect, you can explain that to your client and use tools to reverse the risk.

For example, if you are starting out, you are often just price testing at a minimal viable product mode. This means you do the minimum at first so you can test what you sell with actual buyers. Here's a guaranteed formula: you go to a client and say, "If you buy this product, at any time in the process or after the process, you can always ask for 100 percent of your money back. My goal is to exceed your expectations. I want you to know you are in good hands."

It's a simple, yet effective, way to diminish the risk for the buyer as you are building your product. I even went one step further when I first developed my consulting business. I wanted to learn about the pain points of my ideal client and create a structure to show how I offer my services. Problem was, I had no idea what I was doing. So when a client asked me what I sell, I told them, "I have a $10,000 consulting package. I want you to buy it. But guess what? You don't need to pay right now. I'll let you know when I've spent enough hours with you and want to stop. After I've delivered value and increased your sales, you can decide if it was worth it."

Why did I do that? Simple: for me, the value came from the opportunity to learn. Also, it was a chance to build self-esteem. I didn't offer my services for free; I simply delayed the invoicing. It made a big difference in mindset.

MAXIMIZING EXISTING PRODUCT VALUE

Take your current product/service/offer at the existing price point. Now, if you are not confident with the value of your product, it's easy to fall into a low-vibration solution. What does that look like? Discounts. You will discount the price point to overcome gaps in perceived value. This has nothing to do with the buyer/client. It's all in the mind of the seller. Here's what goes through your head:

Value < price

Solution: lower price

Value = discounted price

Yet, if you want to step into the love energy, the abundance energy, you need to move the other way. You need to increase the price. Massively. Think even ten times the price. Here is what now happens:

Value < price

Solution: multiply price by ten

Value = tenfold price?

How do we make this last equation true? You need to massively change the offer to match the new price.

You become creative. You become innovative. You'll be amazed at what you can do.

Remember the example I gave with Zentrepreneur? The price of admission for this annual event was $2,000. Problem was, we didn't fit into the market for the client we were able to attract. Some were really stretched to pay that amount but also really wanted to come to the event. Others wanted it to be a VIP gathering and were willing to pay more; they felt like at $2,000, there would be too many people and not enough curation.

Once I had more knowledge about the client, we looked back at the product and thought, *What would it look like if it was a $20,000 offer instead?* We changed the package to include monthly calls, a content library, concierge service, and an overall more premium event.

I included a few crazy ideas in the package as well. One of them was allowing the client to come into the office and sit with any team department to learn their processes and be able to replicate it for their own business.

I remember showing my idea to Vishen Lakhiani, the founder of Mindvalley, and he said, "Wait, this is a little extreme. I don't think we have the capacity to execute everything here."

I reassured him that this was not the time to measure the possibility. This was simply a brainstorm to come up with radical ideas. That's the point. When you increase the price by ten times, you have to really get creative without restrictions. So when you start thinking about structuring a product that will work, you'll have more options on the table beyond "let's cut the price."

Here's the last step. If you are going to be brainstorming boldly with possibilities, don't forget to think of radical ways to reverse the risk. In other words, think about all the hesitations someone would have about investing time, money, and energy into your offer. Now think of all the ways you can eliminate these doubts, even if it would come out of your pocket. Remember, with a significantly higher price, your profit margins would be massive! You could take many more calculated risks yourself to ensure the conversions happen.

For example, if someone hesitated to pay $20,000 for an event, what could you add to encourage them? Maybe something like, "If you buy it now, attend the event, apply all the ideas you learned, and still didn't make at least $100,000 more from it, you can get a full refund! We will even put that in writing."

Crazy, right? Again, I'm not saying necessarily to do it. I'm saying you can start to put those creative ideas on paper to make sure you come from a place of abundance.

This is what happens when you love your product so much that you can refashion it in a way that drives value and impact to the clients in massive ways.

Now, of course, once you come back to earth, you'll start to notice a few things:

1. You might find that some of the ideas you came up with could be done with the existing product. You realize that they don't cost much and would allow you to drive the perceived value and the real value to a point where you can better sell your product now.

2. You might have seen ways that the real value and perceived value went up so much that you might now consider charging a premium for your product.

3. You might also realize that the exercise has allowed you to come up with a completely new premium product at a much higher price point. This could be offered to top clients.

All of these are positive outcomes. It's a great process in which to reframe yourself.

When I did this exercise, I found I could add elements to change the price to $7,500. It became the most profitable division of the company and included some of the happiest clients as well.

At the core of every sale, there is a client who will own and experience your product. If you ensure that you love your product, you'll try your hardest to make the best possible version, and you continuously look for ways to improve the value and reduce costs, thereby reaching higher profit margins.

Your profit margin does nothing for the client. The guilt you might feel about your high profit margin is merely about you and will only make you resist selling. When you focus on the real value and the perceived value—as long as they are higher than the price—this is what matters to the client.

The higher the profit, the more you can reinvest in the company to grow, make a bigger impact, and keep some abundance for yourself, too. The world needs you to have a profitably operational business to continue to deliver your impact, serve your client, and make the product.

Now we are going to step into what I believe is the most exciting chapter of this whole book: Love the Process. This is where we challenge every idea around manipulation and acknowledge that what you are really doing is showing a whole lot of love, one sale at a time.

ACTION STEPS

1. Make a list of all the reasons you would hesitate to sell your product. This can be any limitations in quality, services, price, reliability, and so forth.

   a. For each item identified, imagine what the worst-case scenario would be if that were to truly happen (e.g., you sell your product and it breaks on the first day. How would your brand be affected?).

   b. Make a list of actions you would have to take for each of these scenarios.

   c. Make a list of actions you can take to prevent these scenarios from happening.

1. To step into a creative, abundant, and loving space, imagine your product/service is being sold for ten times the price. What features would you add to it to ensure its value exceeded the price?

   a. Once that list of features is complete, think about how you can integrate some of them into your current offer. You may decide to raise the price even more.

b. If this new offer at ten times the price seems appealing, see if anyone wants to buy it.

CHAPTER 8

LOVE YOUR PROCESS

"We don't need any sales or marketing. Everything sells from word of mouth."

Every time I hear this, I cringe. I think it's the most fear-based statement that businesses use to justify their mediocre performance and to avoid the benefits of selling with love.

It's very damaging because you deny a core part of your business operations. If your business is alive and people are buying (even through word of mouth), then you already have marketing and sales happening. You are just not acknowledging it.

I often find myself reading a book full of the kinds of topics most of these people would find offensive.

- *Sell or Be Sold: How to Get Your Way in Business and in Life* by Grant Cardone

- *Influence: The Psychology of Persuasion* by Robert Cialdini

- *Getting Everything You Can Out of All You've Got: 21 Ways You Can Out-Think, Out-Perform, and Out-Earn the Competition* by Jay Abraham

- *SPIN Selling* by Neil Rackham

- *The Sales Acceleration Formula: Using Data, Technology, and Inbound Selling to Go from $0 to $100 Million* by Mark Roberge

- *The Challenger Sale: Taking Control of the Customer Conversation* by Brent Adamson and Matthew Dixon

- *The 48 Laws of Power; The Art of Seduction;* and *The Laws of Human Nature* by Robert A. Greene

If I put all those books in a stack and handed it over to anyone with a negative attitude toward sales, they see it as a confirmation of the evil and manipulation that exists in sales.

Yet, you'll soon realize this is a big mistake. None of these books are evil. We talked earlier about the four stages of emotions in selling. If someone is still in the fear-pride paradox, they will be susceptible to being manipulative. In that case, these books could be like throwing gasoline on a burning house. Loving the process happens only after loving the impact, buyer, and product. Once you are doing business from a place of love and trying to make the world a better place, it's now time to apply love to the process that will lead to increased sales.

Learning about sales techniques when you operate from a place of love isn't manipulative. It's empathetic.

SPEAKING TO REAL PEOPLE

I have a theory. It's a way I think about how I make decisions. I also feel this is a way most people seem to behave when they make their own decisions. Our logical mind, found in the prefrontal cortex, is actually the most recent part of the brain that evolved. Underneath it is the more "lizard brain" we evolved from. I feel like all information we absorb passes through these more primitive parts of the brain before ultimately reaching the logical, rational part of the mind in the prefrontal cortex. As a result, everything coming in is "filtered" by these more primitive parts. It creates a sort of distortion. And that intense distortion, I feel, is made up of our emotions.

When I'm faced with data, I first filter it through how I "feel" about the information. And as the data I allow to pass gets analyzed, I also make my final decisions by seeing how this newly analyzed data "feels" to me.

In a sense, emotions are the gatekeepers of decisions. This is why I often see clients express things like, "Well, it doesn't feel right."

The mistake some sellers will make is to provide more external "proof" in the sales process that the product is worth buying. However, sometimes this doesn't address the client's internal feelings, which are the most important factors.

Isn't that a shame? You have an amazing product that truly serves, yet you are unable to deliver the impact because you don't speak the same language as your buyer. This actually holds your success back. It also holds the buyer's experience back, and if you did all the previous steps right, it holds the entire planet back from receiving your gift. What you need is a translator to raise your perceived value in the eyes of the client. If you learn more about the process of selling, you can make sure the person understands and takes action.

Let's go back to the formula.

If your real value is very high, yet the perceived value is below the price, the sale that *should've* happened did not.

But guess what? The need will still be there. Only the seller who is able to offer a perceived value that is higher than the price will get the sale, *regardless* of the true value.

Sure, in the long term, sellers who grossly inflate perceived value might later get bad reviews, ultimately bringing down the perceived value. However, do you understand the cost of that to everyone? When you haven't raised your perceived value high enough, you are now leaving the client to suffer and buy elsewhere. They might be manipulated and taken advantage of, when you could've brought them into your business and taken good care of them.

I use this extreme scenario to stir you. To challenge you. The process of selling can be such an exhilarating topic. Isn't it liberating to know so many resources exist to help you speak the language of your buyers? You've done the work to build a great product with love, and now you can serve the people you cared enough about to understand.

Let's break down the major parts of the sales process. This beautiful way to look at all its elements will show you what happens when you sell from a place of love.

A Golden Opportunity: The Sale after the Sale

A lot of people see only half of a sale's glory. People put so much effort into closing the sale, making sure to have the best marketing material, and studying everything to maximize conversion. The buyer is feeling the "love" and decides to buy.

But what about afterward? Once the purchase is done, you might forget about them and move to the next buyer. This would be fine… if you had an account manager who would continue to take care of them. More often than not, the amount of effort put into "selling" a buyer after a purchase pales in comparison to the effort of getting them in.

If this were like dating, it would be the one-night-stand method of sales. You close, you move on, you don't care, you ghost. That's not selling with love.

I love the quotes that share how successful relationships are about cherishing your partner every day, just like you did the day you met them. The sale after the sell is what separates the great from the merely good salespeople.

When you put that same amount of energy into your existing clients and continue to deliver a great experience, you'll see that this is the secret to really turning your customers into raving fans. A raving fan will bring you more growth and business than you can imagine. It's also the one place where you will have less competition. You will stand out more because no one else is doing as much. Most other people are just trying to sell their stuff in any way possible.

Be the best salesperson you can—truly show what love is—by taking the time to map out the sales process *after* the purchase is made. How is your team welcoming the new client? What surprises can you give this person as a client? How can you tailor the experience to provide moments that are truly memorable? These are questions you can ask yourself to make the process of selling even more an expression of love.

THE DARK SIDE OF SALES PROCESSES

Now, when does sales become manipulation? You know that there are many examples of sales that take advantage of people. You see techniques that make you think, *Oh wow, that sounds a little awful!*

Wouldn't it be nice to have a litmus test, a way of knowing right from wrong? Luckily, there is one. Remember when we took the time to justify your impact? Here's what we're going to do now.

First, break down everything you have in place to support the sale of your products and services. You want to be able to write down the purpose of each system, item by item. Let's use a classic example here. A car salesman will offer to buy you a drink from the vending machine, just before it's time to buy. The purpose? You, the client, feel like you "owe" it to them to buy the car, just because they bought you a drink. It's a psychological technique of influence.

Is it wrong? Is it manipulative? Where do you draw the line?

The test is simple. You've written down all your sales techniques and why each process exists. Now look at your first one. Imagine that your client has already bought your product. Could you honestly tell them to their face how you used this technique and why?

That's the ultimate test. It's like a magician revealing their secret to the audience once the trick is done. Everyone loves to see a rabbit disappear from the hat. But if they knew you killed the rabbit to make that trick happen, I'm not sure they would keep coming to the show.

Think of all your sales tactics as temporary secrets you must reveal after the sale is closed. How would your client feel upon learning about them? Used? Impressed? If you're not immediately sure, then imagine making those disclosures to a happy client. This will give you the information you need.

In the world of internet marketing, we often run ads for free training, which then leads to the sale of a product. If you explained that process to the buyer, they would naturally find it impressive.

"If you're looking for inspiration, ideas, and growth, we'll show you an ad on Facebook or Google. We offer a free training for forty minutes on that topic, and when the training is over, we suggest you purchase a full course about it. Four percent of the people buy, and the 96 percent of the people who don't still got to learn something."

Not bad, right?

Ask yourself that question constantly: can I comfortably share my process with my customer after the sale? Be as detailed as you can about each step of the process. Not only will it help you understand why you do what you do, but your buyers will appreciate your process more. You'll have that test to make sure you don't step into the dark side. As a bonus, you'll have training material for your sales reps, and they'll be more excited about using the techniques.

Loving the process is so fun because the world of optimizing marketing and sales is truly massive. You can identify any problem you have in the company and ask yourself the question, "How can I address this from a place of love?"

One recent phenomenon in the space of digital marketing has been the trend toward giving more value for free. Giving value, as opposed to producing loads of content without meaningful value, has become one of the highest return on investment (ROI) activities to build a brand, expand the traffic, and convert leads into customers. Search engine tools like Google are giving people what is considered the highest value for their questions. This can lead to the trap of "let's write an article like this so that we capture traffic for those keywords." I've fallen into this trap before.

It usually leads to pretty mediocre results. The question should never start with the conversion. The article needs to be written with the idea of thinking "how can I help the client solve a problem?" Once you answer that question, only then can you look at the process of SEO and so forth.

Remember: Everything you create is a product first. Only after the product is filled with love do you move over to loving the process, and then optimizing it for traffic and conversions.

THE ABCS OF SELLING

Remember this story? Standing in a small, closed office with no windows at 8:00 a.m., I'm here with my two junior sales reps. We are about to hit the phones for another day of "inbound sales activities." I'm in my early twenties. We start the day watching that scene from *Glengarry Glen Ross* when Alec Baldwin shares what it requires to do real estate.

"It takes brass balls."

We get hyped up. Then he shares the age-old ABCs of selling:

"Always. Be. Closing."

After that scene, we jump on the phones to make hundreds of calls for that day, feeling energized and enthusiastic. There is some fun truth in Baldwin's statement. Humans are emotional beings. We don't always act in rational ways. As a salesperson, asking for the close multiple times will indeed increase your sales numbers. Yet, I'd like to change this up a little so we don't forget a critical part of the process:

Always. Be. Caring.

Caring is more important than the closing. It's sometimes uncomfortable to challenge the beliefs of the buyer to help them understand the value of a product. Often, salespeople give up on a sale just to avoid this discomfort. But if they care, discomfort is easily overcome. Their driving focus is now on how to improve the buyer's life with the product in their hands.

I hear people say, "I'm never pushy in a sale." It's the most disingenuous thing I ever hear. Have you ever tried to drag a friend to the gym? Or convinced them *not* to buy that ice cream in an emotional moment? I've had times when I've gone crazy trying to drag someone out of bed to come hiking. Why? They said they wanted to the night before, and now, as they lie in bed feeling lazy, they feel like giving up on themselves. Yet, you go out of your way because you care.

Don't let your own discomfort get in the way of the conversion.

DON'T SABOTAGE YOUR SALE!

Many times in the process of selling, we get in our own way. I want you to remember a simple acronym of feelings to check if they arise. This is to ensure you can always come from a place of love when you sell a product or service.

Scared

We talked already about fear as a common response to sales. When you find yourself scared to pick up that phone, send that email, or work on that campaign to sell more, there is a clue here. You want to make sure you can step forward with confidence. Being scared will drag you down.

If you catch yourself with this feeling, make a fear list. What are you afraid of? Take a few deep breaths, write it out. See how much of the fear is coming from stories you tell yourself. Is it rejection? Is it the responsibility that comes with the sale?

You've already done the work for the first four loves in selling. You are on the right path and should not be afraid to move forward boldly.

Arrogant

Do a quick self-check. Are you condescending to the buyer? Are you coming off with an air of superiority? Do you think the buyers are stupid and you need to "fix" them?

I can assure you that this will not result in a fun sales process. If you remember the discussion of pride in selling from Chapter 3, you already know this attitude will not create lasting results. Do a self-audit here and think about how to communicate with the best intentions in mind. I'm not saying you can't be firm. But there is a fine line between strong language to direct powerful action (think Tony Robbins.) and being an asshole (oops.).

Begging

Do. Not. Beg. For. A. Sale. You have much more dignity than that. You might be able to squeeze a sale from someone who will "pity" you. But rest assured, they will avoid your calls and not feel excited to see you.

We talked about bringing massive value to the buyer. If you did all the steps right, they should be begging *you* to take their money for the impact you will make in their lives from the purchase.

Ordinary

When I first shared this SABO concept publicly, I got to the O... and froze in the presentation. It was a new concept that I had not presented before. I was so embarrassed that I told the audience, "Um, I'll get back to the O at the end of the presentation."

Great, I thought, *this is going to buy me some time to remember.* I continued with the presentation, and when I finished, I had forgotten to come back to that last letter, O.

When the question period started, one of the attendees asked, "What is the O? You never told us."

I admitted I had forgotten and needed to go to my notes. I wasn't very proud of that moment, yet once I took a glance, I was in shock and started laughing.

I had forgotten that the O stood for "ordinary." I just couldn't remember this word for the life of me. Ironically, the whole presentation became an example of exactly what happens when you make sales this way:

When you are being ordinary, you are not remembered.

How do you show up with that extra energy? How do you make that sales process special? What are you doing to stand out from the competition? See what happens when you do a gut check and discover ways to be extraordinary while selling.

SELLING IN THE ONLINE ERA

Back in the early 2000s, the exponential growth of the internet was among us. I remember hearing and reading articles asserting that the salesperson was going to be replaced with online sales. Marketplaces like eBay and Amazon were gaining momentum. The future was viewed as one in which you could buy everything from a car to a house, all with a few clicks of a button. The annoying salesperson would disappear.

Fast-forward twenty years, and I see the role of the salesperson has become more critical than ever. People imagined a world of perfect access to information, but we have faced a reality of information overload. An era without a need for salespeople is an imaginary world where people make decisions from a purely rational perspective, as opposed to an emotional one. But that is far from how things work in reality. To help buyers, we have new ways of selling to inform, instruct, and guide them to make decisions, and the modern salesperson must blend in these online marketing elements.

For instance, in direct response sales, you can actually automate your sales processes to happen at scale. You'll see people make videos on YouTube, Instagram, and Facebook, write blog articles, post on LinkedIn, and employ many other strategies to create content. By doing so, you can establish yourself as an authority in the process. You'll see people create funnels, landing pages, webinars, product launches, sales pages, and more to convert visitors into sales. You'll use ads, remarketing, surveys, direct messaging, and e-commerce.

These are all ways in which the process of selling has moved online. It's a beautiful thing. It allows for scale, predictability, and reaching new markets in ways thought impossible before. Entire books have been written on each of the topics I mentioned above, as the world of online marketing is massive. If you are in love with the process (which by this time, you should be), then you'll naturally get curious about this. They represent very effective ways to maximize sales to the largest group possible. Again, when you've applied the love of the impact, client, and product, the process of learning new ways to reach the people is always coming from a place of empathy and understanding.

You can be selling online or offline, but the principles of the sale are the same. You are looking to maximize perceived value so the purchase is made. You want to study the triggers of influence, human psychology, and any sales tactics or strategies that will make people see why your product/service is amazing.

IMPROVING YOUR PROCESS WITH MARKET RESEARCH

One of the best tools I've used over the years is something called the Net Promoter Score (NPS). This is a simple question sellers ask to evaluate their customers' happiness:

How likely would you be to recommend your product or service to another customer?

The customer answers on a 1–10 scale with optional commentary below. When the seller calculates the score at the end, they find the percentage of promoters (those who give a score of 9 or 10) minus the detractors (those who score 0–6).[11]

---

11 "What Is Net Promoter?" https://www.netpromoter.com/know/.

Anything above 0 is good. Anything over 50 is amazing.

Most people merely look at this tool as a way to improve the product. However, there is so much more you can do with this data that can show love in a big way. Here are some ideas.

Identify the Promoters and Talk to Them

When you find out who all the promoters are, get on the phone with them and ask why they loved your product so much. These are the people you want your sales team and marketing team to connect with, too. There is nothing more wasteful than a salesperson who has become disconnected from loving the impact of their work. Getting your team to speak to the promoters will make them understand the customer more. It will also reignite a flame in their souls to start selling again with better engagement. The best part? You'll be able to pick up testimonials, case studies, and stories you can use in future sales as well.

Identify the Detractors and Let Your Customer Support Team Try to Understand Them

Don't let your sales team talk to the detractors. It will confuse them unless they can fully keep in mind that some of these people are *not* your ideal client. That is what your customer support team is for.

Part of loving your client is to actually know which ones will likely never receive real value above the price from your product. Come with this attitude: "It's not you; it's me." It's like going on a date with someone only to realize that you are both looking for very different things and have very different preferences.

You'll want to identify areas that could be quick fixes in the product and the process while talking to them. For example, listen to a customer who complains about a feature you can fix easily. You'll get all the data you need right then. Plus, when you reach out to these people, you send the message that they were heard. Most of these people simply want to be heard.

As I explained in Chapter 6, "Love Your Client," you have to be careful not to change your product just to satisfy the people who aren't your ideal customer. After you've established your target "ideal client," this doesn't mean you need to make every person fit that ideal. If you try to satisfy everyone, no one will feel special. Not everyone is a fan of Justin Bieber, for example, and that's perfectly okay.

Here's an example of listening to your detractors without diluting the uniqueness of your product. Back in March 2020 when COVID-19 started escalating around the world, a massive shift to working from home was in effect. There was no time to prepare for the shift and people were looking for answers on the fly. Luckily, I had been working from home for years already, and I was asked to put together a course on the topic. In my style of work, I use tools and technology as pillars to productivity (from home or not).

Some students who didn't use any of the technology I recommended started to complain. I listened to them. Afterward, I edited my sales page, adding a line that said, "This product will teach you how to best use technology from your laptop or desktop. If you don't feel like learning how to use technology, this course isn't for you."

Two things will happen. First, the detractors will self-select and not buy the course. Next, more of the ideal target promoters will be excited about getting exactly what they want: a course that will teach them how to use technology. Win-win.

Read the Comments

The gold is found in the data. All those comments allow you to identify priorities that will make the product better. Take the time to read, understand, and digest the rich information being offered by commenters.

This is a powerful process that allows you to spread goodness all around. Never lose connection to the client.

A WHOLE NEW WORLD TO LOVE

A good friend of mine, Hanson, once invited me to do this crazy martial art training with him: Brazilian Jiu-Jitsu. When he first approached me with the idea of fighting with other people on the ground—sort of like wrestling, all sweaty and absolutely getting inside my personal space—my answer was simple: no way.

Yet, there were two special things about my friend that I already knew, relevant to this story. First, I had lots of respect for him and how he lived his life. He is a very smart businessman who has designed a great personal life with his partner, and they have amazing dogs, Pickles and Bella. I've relied on him in the past for recommendations on setting up a studio. I was extremely happy with what he had suggested, and I trusted his opinion.

Second, he had a special kind of persistence about this Jiu-Jitsu thing. He talked about it every time I saw him. He always offered me a free trial, saying, "You want to come try it?" or "You want to join me tomorrow?" Yet, I never found it annoying. It was always intriguing. And always done in such an authentic way.

One day, I decided I'd suspend my negative preconceptions of this martial art and give it a try. My first class was…well…very awkward. Everything I was afraid of happened. During the warm-up drills, people were doing rolls and moves that I hadn't done since I was a child. Looking awkward and running into others, I was already embarrassed. When we started to learn the moves, I felt weirded out by the proximity needed when you are holding someone down or being held down yourself. We got sweaty, I couldn't defend myself, and I felt a little ridiculous.

Yet, the community there was very supportive. The trainings focused on the basics. The sweatiness and proximity wasn't a big deal by the end of it. In the end, I truly came to realize the benefits of this sport. I felt present. I was grounded. I was recharged. It made me more aware of how my body and mind work together. It's been so powerful in my life that I continue to make it a practice and, in the process, reap all the benefits. Me? Jason? A Jiu-Jitsu guy? I guess so.

I'm so happy Hanson applied some basics of *Selling with Love* in the process (however unknowingly). It opened up this whole new world of possibility and provided tools to support my self-growth and self-mastery.

Now that you are learning about sales, in your future studies you'll be excited to hear about all the amazing tools and methods that exist to become better at sales yourself. You'll be able to learn about closing techniques, the prospecting idea, branding, social media marketing, copywriting, and so much more. You'll discover technology that enables you to be more effective in selling—the whole nine yards. Just like how I started in martial arts, it may feel uncomfortable at the beginning. Rest assured that with an open mindset and the right environment, you'll be able to learn and master this new skill. It's a big world with much to explore. When you do it for love, it's an exploration that is absolutely worth it.

As a result of writing this book, I decided to create such an environment for others to continue learning the ways of selling. It's a community that supports the discovery of effective sales methods that are done with integrity. You can find details about it by going to jasonmarccampbell.com/process.

Here's the biggest takeaway from this fourth step, loving the process: become passionate about your technique. The more you learn about sales, human psychology, and marketing, the more you speak the language that is necessary for people to understand your value. It's the empathic language needed to get people to let go of the status quo, check that fear of the unknown, and take a leap of faith with you. Knowing how you worked so hard on making the first three loves clear, you shouldn't hold back on this one either.

One thing to keep in mind which is particularly apparent for this love: Love takes time for love to grow. It's with practice, experience, trial and error, exposure, and all the fun that comes with having faith in the process. I promise as you go on this journey, you'll experience success in selling. As these beautiful memories are created, you'll see yourself falling more and more in love with the process of selling.

If there is still any resistance to selling at this point, it will be resolved by what I believe is the love that heals all other loves. They say you should save the best for last. Well, this one is going straight to the heart, and we won't hold back.

ACTION STEPS

Complete the following Loving the Sales Process Audit.

Rate yourself from 1 to 5 (strongly disagree to strongly agree) on the following statements:

1. I have more leads than I can handle.

2. I know my conversion metrics across my sales pipeline.

3. I can accurately forecast my sales numbers each month.

4. I have a well-documented sales book to support myself and my sales team.

5. I have the right technology to support myself and my sales team to close more.

6. Once a buyer purchases, I know they are in good hands and will become a raving fan.

7. I feel confident in the way we sell. I bring the best from myself and my team, and we treat clients very well.

Then notice the elements that you did not rate a 5. See what it would take to make it a 5. And start working on these elements.

CHAPTER 9

LOVE YOURSELF

With the more technical, practical applications of using love to maximize your sales behind us, this next chapter brings it back to the self. Maybe this chapter feels unnecessary. And sure, you can sell and drive revenue with the first four loves. Yet to sell in a consistent, harmonious manner, this chapter is critical. Loving yourself is how we deal with the hard times.

Sales is great when things are going well. In sales, as in life, you'll find that there are some moments you are in flow. Things are going according to plan. You get out of bed in the morning with clarity of impact. You know who the ideal client is, and you have the energy to serve. Your product is the best it can be in the moment, and your sales "machine" is well optimized.

Then the first sales call you make that day is with a new client who starts with this:

"I can't believe you took my money! You are a manipulating thief, and your product is a piece of shit! I'm going to write terrible reviews about your product, your business, and about you!"

DEALING WITH NEGATIVE SALES INTERACTIONS

Not so fun. Depending on how you let it affect you, you might find yourself in a slump for the rest of the day. When the buyer throws lots of negative energy at you, you might internally react in different ways:

- I'm so sorry! Please, please don't write a review like that.

- How dare you! You're just so stupid, you don't know how to use it!

- I'll just give you your money back and tell you to never buy here again.

- Actually, I'm not a manipulative person. You are the one who didn't follow all the instructions I gave you.

The beauty in sales is that you can always choose how to react to anything that comes your way. If we go back to our four suboptimal emotions while selling, do you see how these responses come from the mindsets of guilt, shame, or reason?

Can you anticipate how ineffective each reaction would be toward your goals for impact?

Selling with love requires higher emotional intelligence.

Let's do the work to make this better. We talked about the four levels of emotions in sales. What I realized is that on a fundamental level, if the guilt and shame still remain, nothing else that is taught matters. You will always regress to your lowest vibration unless you apply energy to counter it. And that is a problem in itself, because energy is a limited resource. If you need to "use" energy to stay at high emotions, you will drain the battery. You'll find yourself dealing with waves of emotions that take you up and down. You need to heal, not push down the blocks that hold you back.

Oh, I wish this was a simple prescription! This last chapter is the most fascinating in the book. There are so many ways to slice the dimension of self-love and work around those blocks. But here is some encouraging wisdom for salespeople.

REGULATING YOUR EMOTIONS
IS THE WAY TO HEALING

One of the key fears I had in sales was bothering people. I remember often picking up the phone and feeling like I was about to commit a crime. Calling a stranger? *How dare I! I'll bother them! They will judge me. They will find out who I am and tell everyone how ridiculous I am.*

The stories my mind would create were quite creative. This is why you will need a level of trust in the process. I remember the very first call I did. I was so nervous dialing the number. I didn't want them to answer. I let it ring. No one picked up. After three rings, I'm thinking of hanging up, but then someone answered.

"Hello?"

Remember the script! I kept thinking to myself. I looked at my notes and I went for it.

"Hi, Ms. Jones. This is Jason from Martel Real Estate. I wanted to let you know that I got your request for a list of hot properties, and we will be emailing it to you in the next twenty-four hours. Is that okay?"

Yes! I did it! At this point, I was trained to expect the lead to acknowledge the courtesy call with gratitude. This would give me space to continue with my qualifying questions. With her answers to those questions, I'd be able to make the pitch. However, what happened next was not in the plan.

"Oh. Okay. Thanks. Bye."

Click. They hung up.

I was terrified. It didn't physically hurt, but it was a blow to my self-esteem. I had sweat on my forehead. I was embarrassed. It was at this exact moment my new boss blasted open the door to ask me how the first call went. His reaction to my look left him asking the obvious question.

"Oh my God, Jason! Are you okay?"

I wasn't. I didn't want to do this. I wanted to quit right then and there. I told him how the person hung up on me, and he started laughing.

"Jason, I swear, in years of doing this, I don't think that's ever happened to me. I promise this is an exception. Best part is, it will never get worse than this! Try another five calls and see what happens."

I picked up the phone and called the next person. This time, they were nice to me. I did it again. The person asked to call later. On the next call, the person booked an appointment.

I got over my fear of bothering people through *repetition*. This forces you to face your fears in rapid succession and overcome them in the process. If you are an aware salesperson, then you already know that with each encounter, you have an opportunity to grow. The lessons from each sales interaction let you become a little more aware of who you are each time.

You want to focus on how to react to each outcome. Let's say the client doesn't want to talk to you, gets mad at you, wants something you can't offer, loves you, buys from you, doesn't buy from you. There are so many outcomes that could result from each interaction, and you need to prepare your reaction to each of these. How do you stay loving and filled with compassion in the moments of "negative" outcomes? How do you manage to stay humble and not get complacent when you have "positive" outcomes?

Just like any other skill you develop, practice makes progress. I'll be the first to judge myself during times I feel inadequate. I feel like I'm not doing my "best." But I'm quick to remind myself to have some self-compassion and patience. One of the pieces of advice that has really stuck with me over the years comes from don Miguel Ruiz. In his book *The Four Agreements: A Practical Guide to Personal Freedom*, he writes about how we all have access to only one action in our lives: always doing our best.[12]

As much as I want my path to growth to be linear and on an upward trajectory at all times, I've seen my life unfold more like a series of cycles. As I remind myself of the advice from above, I take moments in the "down" times to appreciate and respect the cycle and to focus on what I can do in the moment. Even if it doesn't feel like my ideal "best," it's the best for now. This is perfectly fine.

If you feel like you need to behave like a famous salesperson in a movie to be a great salesperson, you are wrong. Especially in our current world where people want truth and authenticity, showing up as yourself is the best sales advantage.

DEALING WITH HESITATION IN SALES

You'll often hear that sales is nothing more than a numbers game. You hear that making more phone calls, scheduling more meetings, and reaching out to more leads will equal more success. There is

---

12 Don Miguel Ruiz and Janet Mills, *The Four Agreements: A Practical Guide to Personal Freedom* (San Rafael, CA: Amber-Allen Publishing, 1997).

some truth to this. Sure, you could argue that waiting to find the right lead is better than going after anybody. Yet, I find most people use this as an excuse to call less, rather than a targeting strategy. Hesitation is what kills the success of a salesperson more than anything. That reluctance to pick up the phone wastes precious time.

There's a beautiful scene from the movie *The Pursuit of Happyness* starring Will Smith as Chris Gardner, a medical equipment salesman. Chris optimizes every little moment in between his calls to make the most per hour. This is where the argument for the numbers game makes sense. If you want to close more deals, take more action. Even when you start, you might not have "the perfect leads"; that's okay. What you lose in immediate quality, you gain in learning.

Imagine getting the opportunity to talk to people who are not yet ready for your solution. You learn more about the client (a chance to express love of the client, right?), and you might even see new product opportunities that would be good for these people (love your product, right?). The more action that happens, the more results and lessons come. Hesitation, on the other hand, is the friction that will stop the flow. Why do we hesitate? This has a lot to do with the fears that hold us back in the sales process, including one of the biggest for early-stage salespeople: the fear of rejection.

No one enjoys being rejected. It can trigger wounds from our childhood, and it can make us feel like we will be punished for not doing the right thing. Yet, the beauty in sales is that for every no you receive, you will live another day to learn from it and grow. You will face yourself and your fears in the process of sales faster than most professions out there. The good news is that because you have a high activity count (calls per hour, meetings per day, depending on your industry), you'll grow that much faster in the process.

HOW MUCH MONEY IS TOO MUCH MONEY?

When I was growing up, I'd organize these parties. Every time I did, I'd create really cool themes and plan for lots of people to come together. I'd even individually message everyone so they felt personally invited and special. I'd get lots of people showing up, and I'd make it an open bar and provide drinks for everyone.

And I would charge ten dollars.

I'd use all that money for the party, and even sometimes run into a loss, because I was so focused on making sure people had a great time. I also felt a sense of guilt if I charged my friends too much. Some of my "cheapest" friends didn't even want to pay the cost. They would assume I made a profit and even called me out, saying, "I bet you make money with this!"

It was sad because, well, I didn't. And deeper than that, I felt that if I did make money, I would be a bad person. I carried the belief that if I made too much money, people would resent me, would not love me, and therefore, I should find ways to give it all away. However, even though charity is an important thing, it shouldn't be done from a place of guilt, as we learned through this book. How do I make a decision from a place of love and choose abundance for myself at the same time? Is that selfish?

Absolutely not. As a matter of fact, *not* choosing abundance is selfish, because you become an example to others that doing good in the world shouldn't be rewarded. When you become abundant as a result of doing good in the world, this is a great thing.

If you followed this book so far, you've made sure you are coming from a place of love in the way you make an impact, serve your clients, design your products, and sell. It's only fair that people who operate from this perspective are adequately rewarded.

That's why work needs to be done to clear the blocks that might be holding you back.

I remember going to a seminar by Jordan Belfort, the Wolf of Wall Street himself. I won't pass judgment on him for his past, but I will share one thing he mentioned that I think can be applied here, too. He talked about the idea of temperature. Everyone has a level of income that makes them comfortable.[13]

For some, it's $50,000 a year. For others, one million. Some want hundreds of millions. Some want an hourly wage. Some have a consulting fee.

---

13 Jordan Belfort, "The Truth behind His Success: The Wolf of Wall Street," Hotel Istana, Kuala Lumpur, Malaysia, July 30, 2014.

Regardless of your unit of measurement, we all have a number we strive toward for comfort. And I love the concept, because when you are clear on it, you will have a motivation to work really hard to achieve it. Everything suddenly has purpose.

However, when I was younger, I had a problem. I didn't know what number I deserved. I kept thinking about the inequality in the world. I thought about the fact that I'm already in the top 1 percent on the planet. And here I am wanting more. Am I selfish? Is wanting millions wrong? My mind would create so many ideas about deserving the money or not.

At the same time, I also felt like there was something wrong with me for not wanting more. Why was my temperature okay with the number it was at? Why wasn't it bigger? I should be hustling harder!

It's a strange paradox. As you might have noticed in the last paragraphs, all this mental chatter was just that—unproductive chatter.

Here is a statement that will help you with any limitations: holding yourself back from greatness is a selfish act. It's about choosing comfort over conversion. When you live abundantly and do your best in the world, you lift the tide for everyone else around you. Knowing this, you can move forward with grace and ensure that you can support yourself, your family, and your community.

If you are not taken care of, your impact will be limited. And if that impact is important, you are important.

Got Privilege? Good—Use It

That word "privilege" is heavy. It comes with lots of baggage, and as a white male writing this book, I acknowledge that I speak from the position of having it. Again, guess what natural instinct gets in the way of wanting to do good in the world? Feeling guilt about the privilege I received. This was a tough one for me to get over, and I still struggle with it today. Yet, I am reminded to share my thoughts about this with you, too. Privilege can be used to do so much good in the world. Using it to create more equality, to be generous, to be kind. To do things the right way. To jump into social issues and champion them.

I encourage you to take a moment to realize that if you have read this far in the book, understood the ideas shared here, and are able to apply them in your work, you already stand on the shoulders of ancestors who have created a wonderful world of opportunities for us. As you go out and seek this abundance for yourself and those around you, you'll realize that giving will be a natural effect. Don't use privilege as a crutch. Use it as a springboard and do it from a place of love.

SELF-CARE FOR SELF-LOVE

The journey to self-love is actually a journey of a lifetime. You'll fluctuate through a range of emotions for yourself, and you'll need to find acceptance. There are many things I've tested over the years that have allowed me to step into more and more self-awareness and self-mastery, which I'd love to recommend. It would be a book in itself to talk about all the ways to form a habit of growth. What I'd rather do is list some of the more important ideas I think will specifically drive your success in sales.

Daily Sacred Choices

I was lucky enough to come across a program called Lifebook. Call it a highly structured vision board process where you get goals in multiple categories of your life (personal and professional). In the process, they advocate for what they call Daily Sacred. These are things you can do daily to ensure you show up as your best self.[14]

Your performance in sales can vary daily from factors that are out of your control: can't reach people on the phones or a deal falls through due to budget cuts. The list goes on. What you can control are the habits that care for you daily. Some can be very simple to implement. Can you make your bed daily? Meditate for X time? Take a cold shower? Maybe you can read a few pages of a book. Keep a journal, avoid hitting the snooze button, go for a walk, or do push-ups. All these have made it to my sacred choices list at some point. They can become the very habits that support you through the day. Design as few or as many as you can. It's your choice. What tends to happen over time is that you notice the benefits these habits bring to your well-being, physically and mentally. I've also seen my sales

---

14   https://www.mylifebook.com/.

performance improve and remain consistent week after week. These little actions, which by themselves may seem trivial, can make all the difference.

Accountability Group

If you are part of a larger organization working in sales, you'll be exposed to daily and/or weekly sales meetings. This can be a "rah-rah" cheerfest where people talk about their deal pipelines, exciting updates, and/or roadblocks they need to overcome. They can increase motivation and focus for the sales team, yet there is one little piece I feel is missing. It doesn't leave room for full, open, and vulnerable conversations. What you say in public here might be too sensitive and might not be received well among peers or managers who need you to perform at your best. Corporate culture literature now speaks more of the benefits of providing safe, open spaces to discuss real challenges. Yet, I don't feel your accountability, progress, and personal issues should be given fully to the organization to manage.

Instead, I built a separate accountability group with two other people where we can discuss anything on a weekly basis. From setting powerful goals to initiating a weekly "one thing" to talking about our struggles, I've seen us grow so fast and build a bond that I haven't had with many others in my life. We are there for each other.

We are all humans going through ups and downs. If you can find yourself building such a circle with friends, with people you respect who are just as growth-oriented as you, it will go a long way.

ARE YOU GOOD ENOUGH FOR SALES?

I have this internal debate in my own head sometimes. You'll notice that it doesn't come from a place of love but rather a combination of guilt, fear, and justification. There is a part of me that loves the chase. I love setting bigger goals and making more money. Impacting more lives. Yet, there's a disconnect in my impatience to achieve them. I want to do more now.

One train of thought that I get is to push harder. Work harder. Do more. Hustle. At the root of all these "expressions of being" is a similar sentiment: what you are doing now is not enough. Often, this translates mentally to "I am not enough."

I've had the joy to learn from amazing teachers I consider my friends now. One of them is Marisa Peer, an amazing teacher in the field of personal growth. She speaks extensively to this idea of "not-enoughness" as one of the biggest problems we all face right now. Most of the pain, suffering, overcompensation, and disappointments come from this root idea.[15]

This is where I want to propose a different idea. What if everything you are doing right now, wherever you are, is enough? What if the pace you are going at right now is the perfect pace for you?

The times I've "rushed" things were always times that I cut corners. I didn't focus on the impact, the client, the product first. Instead, I

---

15 Marisa Peer, *I Am Enough: Mark Your Mirror and Change Your Life* (self-pub., June 2018).

looked for processes that got me results faster. When I do this, I come from a place of scarcity. (Remember the fear-pride paradox from Chapter 3?)

I believe many of the problems we see in the world today stem from this idea of being impatient with the results. What we are saying in times we demand results faster is "I don't trust the universe." In response to this, I'll bring up a quote frequently attributed to Albert Einstein: "One of the most important questions you can ask yourself is: is the universe friendly?"

If you answer yes, then you know that you are on the perfect path made for you and everything will be okay. Look at you, finishing a book on sales, learning so much about how to do it from a place of love! You are now in a growth phase, and you must have trust in the process.

If you answer no, the universe doesn't care, what actions will you take? Will you be indifferent? Fight it? What results would that bring? I have a feeling that the consequent experience will confirm your beliefs about the universe not being friendly...at a terrible cost to you.

Of course, we can't know the answer for sure. Yet, the choice you make of belief is a powerful choice indeed. No matter what religion you are or what faith you have, it all leads to a simple idea: *you are enough.* You are already doing your best, and there is no one you need to compare yourself to.

When you come from that place, you are choosing self-love in a powerful way. And that is huge in the process toward selling more from love.

Vishen Lakhiani, the founder of Mindvalley and my close friend, talks about a concept called blissipline in his book *The Code of the Extraordinary Mind: 10 Unconventional Laws to Redefine Your Life and Succeed on Your Own Terms*. Basically, blissipline (bliss + discipline) is the idea that you need a vision for the future, but you must try to stay happy in the now. Everything we achieved in the first four loves of selling was about getting excited about what you will be creating in the future, painting that vision, and getting clear on the impact. But finally, the work that needs to be done is to be happy in the now.

You are enough, you will always grow, there is no rush, and your first love is self-love. I've kept it last in this book only because I want this to resonate with you and stay with you for the years to come.

It's the final message you need to hear about self-love. Even if you put this book down and decide to never make a sale in your life, you want to apply this self-love to fill your life with joy, presence, and flow. There is no reason to resist the ups and downs of life. Simply take a step back, be fascinated with the learning opportunities and great moments, and you'll be more fulfilled as a result.

ACTION STEPS

1. Do you have any hesitations left when thinking about selling? Can you isolate the fear?

2. Do you have blocks around making money? If so, can you identify the key story you tell yourself?

3. Have a look at your daily habits. See which ones support your growth and which ones hold you back. Can you make small changes?

4. How clear are you on your long-term goals? If not, can you take a moment to go deeper?

5. Are you ready to *Sell with Love*? Good, the world needs it. Write down a statement to remind yourself why you choose to sell with love and why you are the perfect person to get the abundance you deserve.

CONCLUSION

Selling is not easy. It demands energy and believing in yourself constantly. It demands being in a heightened state of enthusiasm and attention, listening and caring about others relentlessly. As we covered in the four emotions of selling in Chapter 3, sometimes we fall back into lower vibrations. We find guilt and shame creeping up on us. At this point, we need to ask ourselves which of the five loves needs attention.

Are you doubting the impact? You can go back to your list to affirm the impact you are making.

Are you doubting your understanding of the client? Call a few more past clients, study your avatar, and get clear on who they are and how to make their lives better.

Are you doubting your product? Review feedback from clients on what can be improved. Run the ten-times-the-price experiment, find ways you can innovate and improve, and do what you can to offer the best product you can.

Are you doubting the process? Read more books on sales. Keep your intentions in check and make sure you cover your first three loves strongly. Then use all the tools that are required to make sure your process is optimized and amazing.

Are you doubting yourself? Remember, you are the perfect one for the task. You have your unique methods and gifts. What you offer to the world is always your best. If you accomplished all the processes from the first four loves, you should pat yourself on the back and recognize that you have done what you can to support others. You deserve abundance, and it is within your grasp. Go out there and serve the world, and don't hold back.

There is a side effect of doing all this work to be a better salesperson. We haven't talked much about it in this book, as the purpose was to educate you to be the best seller possible. Yet, you'll be excited about the power this part of the equation holds.

As you strive to be a better seller, you automatically become a better buyer. If we want to make the world a better place, being better buyers is important, too. The dollars we spend on the things we want is a vote for what we want to see in the world. It's also a vote for what you expect from a salesperson.

Imagine walking into a business and asking them about what personally motivates them to sell. What is the impact they want to make? What research has been done into the perceived customer needs? How can they improve and support the product? What sales processes are in place to reduce risk? These are all powerful questions that are not typically answered in the sales process. Yet, they are the critical questions to identify where this transaction sits on the emotional equation.

As the buyer, how clear are you on what is important to you in the world? What are some changes you wish to see? Did you know that you can be responsible for those changes with every dollar you spend?

I remember walking into a pizza restaurant and seeing all the amazing options on the menu. From all the options available, I noticed that there was a little section with vegan pizza options. Although I admit that a part of me did want to have the satisfaction of burrata cheese on a pizza, I understood that more important to me than my emotional needs for dairy in the moment was the expansion of available vegan options everywhere I go. See, every time I decide to order a vegan dish, I send a signal to the restaurant of the options that make money. Everywhere I go, I get to vote with my dollars. I have to tip my hat to the first people who made this dietary choice and were faced with confused looks when they had to ask, "Can you make this without dairy or meat?" Early-adopter buyers have shaped these market options.

When you take time to be a better buyer, you also get clear on what is important to you, and then you can vote with each purchase in alignment with that.

The world is a beautiful place. With this beauty, there is always the possibility to recognize that things can get better. We can play a part in making that happen. As a role model salesperson who embodies everything in this book, you will be a catalyst for making every energy exchange in the world contain a powerful force of love. You have the power to become more conscious, aware, caring, and aligned with yourself.

ACKNOWLEDGMENTS

MAKING THIS BOOK A REALITY WAS AN EFFORT BY MANY WHO supported me throughout the journey. I've been blessed to have such amazing people come into my life at the right time to support me with what I need, making the whole journey a beautiful experience.

I'd love to first thank my parents, Lyne and Tom. You have been so supportive throughout my life with all the decisions I've made (including the crazy ones). You have never judged me through my tough times, and you have allowed me to build my own path in this world. You are the foundation for who I have become. I am so grateful for this, and I love you very much.

To my sisters, Jamie and Tracy. You are the best siblings I could ask for, and I'm grateful for all the amazing times we had growing up together. I couldn't imagine life without you in it, and even though I'm far away, I'll always feel close to both of you.

Big thanks to Eric Strauss and Ezekiel Vicente. As my accountability partners since 2018, you have been with me along the whole journey of writing this book. Your ability to kick my butt and challenge me when needed has made this possible without driving me crazy. And a special thanks to you, Ezekiel, for coaching me through some of the tougher times. Your wisdom has been a big part of my character today.

I wouldn't be here without the massive support I've gotten from Vishen Lakhiani, founder of Mindvalley. You've always been a big supporter of me, you've always given me many opportunities to shine, and I am so grateful for everything you have done. I also want to extend this thanks to all the present and past people who have been a part of Mindvalley. Getting to work alongside all of you for those years has made me see what happens when you bring together the most amazing people from around the world to do amazing things. I've been shaped by everyone involved there.

I'd love to thank the whole team at Scribe Media. I decided to take a leap of faith to make this book project a reality, and I couldn't have done it without your guidance and support. It's the best decision I ever made, and this book is a result of that decision.

To Cedric Meloche and Marc-André Lalonde. You guys were my first business partners, and we went through thick and thin during those crazy real estate years. I think back on our BSD days, and it was some of the most life-changing growth experiences. You both still support me in huge ways, and I am so grateful for all you do. Brotherhood.

I want to recognize Colton Swabb and Gavin Abeyratne. That fateful trip you made to come visit me in Miami was the catalyst for making me take those steps required to turn my concepts of selling with love into a book. Thank you so much.

I want to recognize a few teachers who've had a big influence on me along the way. Eric Edmeades, you helped me shape my communication ability to a new level and got me to build a body I am very proud of through nutrition education as well. Thank you for the guidance.

Professor Srikumar Rao, thank you for taking me through your Creativity and Personal Mastery Program. This has allowed me to grow in so many ways and build a character I am proud of today.

Jon and Missy Butcher, through your Lifebook Program, you've given me the power to set bold visions and goals in my life. What started as very vague business goals became the clarity to write this book. Thank you for your support.

Aya Jean, your work in doing a transformation with me was so impactful. Thank you for taking a chance on me while I was just a little guy. You built up my confidence, and I always have so much fun with you.

David Szecsei, thank you for being a great friend and one of the most enthusiastic salespeople I know. You are a great example of someone who can balance the caring and the closing in the way I want to inspire so many more people to do.

Chee Ling and Milka, I want to thank you both for jumping in with design help, as you know I struggle with understanding branding from a visual point of view. You've taken my ideas and vision and turned it into a visual language I can use to reach more people.

I'd love to thank the following people who took the time to review my work and provide their support. I'm extremely grateful that you put your trust in me and took the time to support me for this first book that I publish. It meant so much to me: Lisa Nichols, Daniel Marcos, Cameron Herold, Teal Swan, Keith Ferrazzi, Nir Eyal, Perry Marshall, Dorie Clark, and Regan Hillyer.

I also want to share gratitude to some incredible women who have been a part of my life. Writing a book on selling with love comes with learning opportunities I've had in my personal life as well. Who I am today has been shaped by the wonderful memories I cherish from my past, as well as powerful lessons from mistakes I have made. I still feel this section wouldn't be complete if I didn't take a moment to acknowledge you. I'll borrow wisdom from the Ho'oponopono mantra and say this: "I love you, I am sorry, please forgive me, thank you."

I also want to thank Steve Martel for getting me into sales at a young age. You have been an early mentor and introduced me to the world of personal growth and sales. My whole life took a turn with the introduction of real estate as well.

On another note, I will also give blessings to the other unintended mentors I've had during my US real estate ventures. Some of you gave me lessons I wasn't ready to receive. In fact, it was probably not your goal to inspire me, yet the challenges you put me through and the deceptions I've dealt with have nonetheless helped shape the values I hold dear, helping me to ensure others don't need to face the same. So I can thank you as well.

There are many more important people in my life who have helped make this book happen.

I do need to take a moment to thank everyone who has picked up a copy of the book. My truest joy is to see a reader who takes the ideas shared in this book and use them to do sales from a place of love. We all get to play a part in shaping the world in a better way, one sale at a time.

ABOUT THE AUTHOR

Jason Marc Campbell has been a sales leader at Mindvalley for over seven years. He also interviews thought leaders around the globe on topics of leadership, team building, communication, productivity, and embracing authenticity in a commercial world. As an international speaker, he has shared the stage with the likes of Gary Vaynerchuk, Jason Silva, Vishen Lakhiani, Lisa Nichols, and others.

Jason's mission is to transform the world by teaching companies to care. Businesses are tremendous sources of power in a capitalist world. If we can educate companies on the value of responsibility in how they sell, how they market, how they treat their employees, and even how they invest their money, we will shift the very planet into a better place for all.

Jason is also the founder of Impact and Integrity Media, a consultancy firm to support growing leaders and provide strategic guidance for organizations' sales and marketing divisions.